D1124315

The
Vietnamese
Americans

Other books in the Immigrants in America series:

The Chinese Americans

The Cuban Americans

The Italian Americans

The Russian Americans

The
Vietnamese Americans

By Tricia Springstubb

Lucent Books, 10911 Technology Place, San Diego, CA 92127

Library of Congress Cataloging-in-Publication Data

Springstubb, Tricia.
   The Vietnamese Americans / by Tricia Springstubb.
      p. cm. — (Immigrants in America)
Includes bibliographical references and index.
Summary: Discusses the history and political conditions of
Vietnam and examines the situation of Vietnamese refugees,
their immigration, social adjustments, employment, and
contributions to American culture.
   ISBN 1-56006-964-3
1. Vietnamese Americans—Juvenile literature. 2. Refugees—
Vietnam —History—Juvenile literature. 3. Refugees—United
States—History—Juvenile literature. 4. United States—
Emigration and immigration—History—Juvenile literature.
5. Vietnam—Emigration and immigration—History—Juvenile
literature. [1. Vietnamese Americans. 2. Refugees. 3. United
States—Emigration and immigration—History. 4. Vietnam—
Emigration and immigration—History.] I. Title. II. Series.
   E184.V53 S67 2002
   305.895'92073—dc21

2001002968

Copyright © 2002 by Lucent Books, Inc.
10911 Technology Place, San Diego, CA 92127

No part of this book may be reproduced or used in any form or
by any means, electrical, mechanical, or otherwise, including, but
not limited to, photocopy, recording, or any information storage
and retrieval system, without prior permission from the publisher.

Printed in the USA

CONTENTS

Foreword   6
Introduction: The Strength of America   8

Chapter One
Why They Left the Home They Loved So Much   12

Chapter Two
In Search of Safety   24

Chapter Three
Welcome to Freedom Land   40

Chapter Four
Early Challenges to Adjustment   53

Chapter Five
Making It in America   65

Chapter Six
Continuing Challenges   78

Chapter Seven
The Future   89

Notes   100
For Further Reading   103
Works Consulted   104
Index   107
Picture Credits   111
About the Author   112

FOREWORD

Immigrants have come to America at different times, for different reasons, and from many different places. They leave their homelands to escape religious and political persecution, poverty, war, famine, and countless other hardships. The journey is rarely easy. Sometimes, it entails a long and hazardous ocean voyage. Other times, it follows a circuitous route through refugee camps and foreign countries. At the turn of the twentieth century, for instance, Italian peasants, fleeing poverty, boarded steamships bound for New York, Boston, and other eastern seaports. And during the 1970s and 1980s, Vietnamese men, women, and children, victims of a devastating war, began arriving at refugee camps in Arkansas, Pennsylvania, Florida, and California, en route to establishing new lives in the United States.

Whatever the circumstances surrounding their departure, the immigrants' journey is always made more difficult by the knowledge that they leave behind family, friends, and a familiar way of life. Despite this, immigrants continue to come to America because, for many, the United States represents something they could not find at home: freedom and opportunity for themselves and their children.

No matter what their reasons for emigrating, where they have come from, or when they left, once here, nearly all immigrants face considerable challenges in adapting and making the United States their new home. Language barriers, unfamiliar surroundings, and sometimes hostile neighbors make it difficult for immigrants to assimilate into American society. Some Vietnamese, for instance, could not read or write in their native tongue when they arrived in the United States. This heightened their struggle to communicate with employers who demanded they be literate in English, a language vastly different from their own. Likewise, Irish immigrant school children in Boston faced classmates who teased and belittled their lilting accent. Immigrants from Russia often felt isolated, having settled in areas of the United States where they had no access to traditional Russian foods. Similarly, Italian families, used to certain wines and spices, rarely shopped or traveled outside of New York's Little Italy, a self-contained community cut off from the rest of the city.

Even when first-generation immigrants do successfully settle into life in the United States, their children, born in America, often have different values and are influenced more by their country of birth than their parents' traditions. Children want to be a part of the American culture and usually welcome American ideals, beliefs, and styles. As they become more Americanized—adopting western dating habits and fashions, for instance—they tend to cast aside or even actively reject the traditions embraced by their parents. Assimilation, then, often becomes an ideological dispute that creates conflict among immigrants of every ethnicity. Whether Chinese, Italian, Russian, or Vietnamese, young people battle their elders for respect, individuality, and freedom, issues that often would not have come up in their homeland. And no matter how tightly the first generations hold onto their traditions, in the end, it is usually the young people who decide what to keep and what to discard.

The Immigrants in America series fully examines the immigrant experience. Each book in the series discusses why the immigrants left their homeland, what the journey to America was like, what they experienced when they arrived, and the challenges of assimilation. Each volume includes discussion of triumph and tragedy, contributions and influences, history and the future. Fully documented primary and secondary source quotations enliven the text. Sidebars highlight interesting events and personalities. Annotated bibliographies offer ideas for additional research. Each book in this dynamic series provides students with a wealth of information as well as launching points for further discussion.

The Strength of America

The people that we are welcoming today . . . are individuals who can contribute significantly to our society in the future. They are people of talent, they are industrious, they are individuals who want freedom, and I believe they will make a contribution now and in the future to a better America.

—President Gerald Ford, May 1975. In *Vietnamese Americans: Patterns of Resettlement and Socioeconomic Adaptation in the United States.*

In the spring of 1975, tens of thousands of Vietnamese left their homeland bound for resettlement in America. Unlike many immigrants, their leaving was neither joyful nor planned. These were people fleeing for their lives.

Two images from those chaotic days were broadcast around the world and remain symbols of the Vietnamese flight. One is of the line of men, women, and children clinging to the walls and roof of the American embassy in Vietnam's capital city of Saigon, begging American soldiers to airlift them out by helicopter. The other is of a small fishing boat, its deck so crammed with passengers that there is barely room to turn around. The thin, exhausted faces of the travelers, called "boat people," reflect the desperation and hardship of their escape by sea. In both images, the world saw a people grasping after survival and freedom.

The flight from Vietnam was the culmination of centuries of struggle within a divided country. Two twentieth-century conflicts—the French-Indochina War and the Vietnam War—had ravaged the countryside, killing thousands and destroying a way of life. The Vietnam War, in which a half million U.S. soldiers participated, deeply divided the American people. Even as the United States withdrew its troops from Vietnam, a bitter debate raged over whether the costly involvement halfway around the world had been right or wrong.

This divided opinion on the war was reflected in the way Americans felt about the newly arriving immigrants. When Vietnamese began seeking asylum in the United States, they faced a range of reactions. Some Americans rushed to help them; others viewed them with resentment or suspicion. The Vietnamese themselves varied widely in background, education, and skill. Very few spoke English well, and most were forced to leave with little more than what they could carry. Suddenly thrown into a culture so different from their own, how they would fare was uncertain.

Despite these initial obstacles, the story of Vietnamese American settlement has been one of vigorous growth. Their population has expanded from an insignificant number in the 1970s to approximately seven hundred thousand by current estimates. Second and third waves of immigration have swelled their community,

As Saigon fell into the hands of the communists, thousands of Vietnamese fled their country.

The Asian Garden Mall lies at the heart of the bustling "Little Saigon" community in Orange County, California.

making the Vietnamese the fastest-growing segment of the Asian American population. They now comprise nearly 9 percent of that ethnic population, which is itself growing faster than any other group in America. As a result, the 2000 census was printed in four foreign languages, including Vietnamese.

With large settlements in California and Texas and thriving communities from New York City to Seattle, Vietnamese Americans have begun to play an increasing role in American culture. In many urban areas, they have restored and revitalized neighborhoods on the verge of decay.

In Orange County, California, for example, ragged strips of vacant lots and boarded-up stores have been transformed into vibrant Vietnamese communities comprised of thriving restaurants, shops, and temples.

Tran can cu, a Vietnamese phrase meaning hard work and patience, has been essential to these successes and remains the key to hope for the future. Even as their children become more and more Americanized, Vietnamese Americans continue to believe strongly in the value of family and community. Further, the high importance they place on education has translated into impressive achievement in a wide variety of fields, including the sciences and business.

Although the Vietnamese as a whole have adapted to their new country with great success, they have never abandoned their old culture. Their language, foods, customs, and religion traveled to America with them, passing down from one generation to the next generation. As the Vietnamese become a more visible part of American life, their rich culture becomes both better understood and more accepted. As they play a more active role in educa-tion, business, and politics, the Vietnamese continue to win respect for their diligence and resourcefulness, cultural values that are centuries old.

Vietnamese Americans are relative newcomers among America's immigrants, yet they, like so many before them, embrace the nation's ideals and enhance the culture with their unique traditions. In President Ford's 1975 speech welcoming the first Vietnamese arrivals, he concluded that, in the United States, "In one way or another, all of us are immigrants. . . . The strength of America is its diversity."[1]

CHAPTER ONE

Why They Left the Home They Loved So Much

I remember crying twice in my life. The first time was when my father hit me; the second was when I left my country.

—Trung, an American citizen, sixteen years old when he fled Vietnam. In James A. Freeman, *Hearts of Sorrow: Vietnamese American Lives*

In the spring of 1975, Vietnam was living out the last days of a long nightmare. Civil war between the North and the South had divided its people and devastated its countryside. For years, the United States had supported the South with troops and weaponry, yet the Americans had failed to defeat the communist forces of the North. As victory for the North became certain, those Vietnamese who had fought on the side of American troops knew their independent, capitalist way of life was coming to an end. Many feared imprisonment, if not death. Escape, then, became the only solution.

A War with an International Impact

Small, fragile Vietnam seems an unlikely country to be the center of such massive conflict. Yet its internal strife coincided with a period in history known as the cold war, which began shortly after World War II ended, and lasted until the Soviet Union dissolved in 1991. The cold war was essentially a contest between the forces of capitalism, represented by the United States, and those of communism, represented by China and the Soviet Union. The United States treated these two communist countries as persistent threats, intent on overthrowing capitalism and democracy wherever they could. Communism was perilous to the free world, many Americans believed, and had to be contained at all costs. During this period, the "domino theory" ruled American foreign policy. This theory compared the weak nations of the world to a row of dominoes. If one toppled to communism, strategists believed, all would.

The United States saw Vietnam as a pivotal domino. The civil war raging there pitted the communist North against the capitalist South. If the communists won in Vietnam, the reasoning went, the rest of Southeast Asia would be sure to fall to the communists, too. Thus, saving Vietnam became a top priority for the United States.

A Tradition of Resisting Outsiders: The French-Indochina War

Vietnam's role in world politics, though, began decades before the United States became involved there. A number of other countries, including China and France, had tried to exert influence in Vietnam. France's involvement dated back to the 1600s, when Catholic missionaries visited Vietnam. During the eighteenth and nineteenth centuries, when internal wars plagued Vietnam, France supplied aid to the various factions, helping to weaken the country. In 1883 France claimed Vietnam as a colony.

French rule lasted seventy years, reinforcing the economic and political divisions already weakening the country and introducing new ones. By establishing rubber, tea, and coffee plantations, the French helped create a society composed of wealthy estate owners at the top, landlords and government officials in the middle, and, at the bottom, impoverished peasants. By introducing their own elite schools, which were attended for the most part by Catholics, the French further divided the wealthy from the poor.

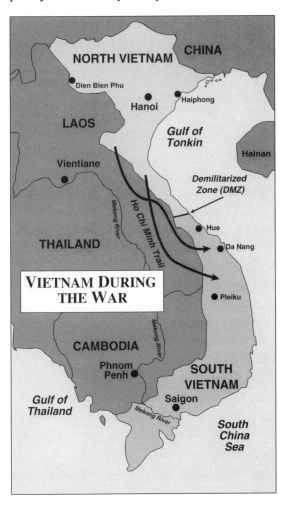

VIETNAM DURING THE WAR

Land of Mountains and Rivers

Vietnam is a country of striking physical beauty. Its variety and richness are vividly described in this selection from Olivia Skelton's book Vietnam: Still Struggling, Still Spirited.

Vietnam is a land of rough mountains, dense forests, and tropical seashores. . . . Most of the country is mountainous. . . . In central Vietnam, swift rivers tumble out of the Central Highlands on their way to the sea, forming waterfalls and deep ravines. Some highlands reach the coast in steep cliffs and seaside hills. Along the coast stretch white, sandy beaches. . . .

Vietnam has many different types of vegetation. Dwarf bamboo trees and needle trees grow in the mountains of the northwest. In the far south, tropical fruit trees, palms, and mangrove forests flourish.

Vietnam has a great variety of wildlife. There are fifty species of mammals, including elephants, rhinoceroses, and tigers. Reptile species include crocodiles and large snakes like the python. Vietnam also has more than 600 species of birds. . . .

During these colonial years, around 1900, many Chinese immigrated to Vietnam as a result of famine and overpopulation in their own country. Most became prosperous businesspeople and merchants, sharing Vietnam's wealth with the French colonizers. Divided and oppressed, Vietnam was ready for a strong leader who would oust the invaders and restore dignity to the peasants.

Ho Chi Minh

The nationalist Ho Chi Minh had been resisting the French for years. His communist coalition, the Vietminh, was a powerful force among the peasants of the North. During World War II, when Vietnam was invaded by Japan, Ho Chi Minh led the Vietnamese resistance against these newest conquerors.

After the end of World War II and the subsequent defeat of Japan, Ho Chi Minh's forces once again took on the French, who were trying to reassert their power in the country. The battle between the French and communist forces became known as the French-Indochina War. It lasted from 1946 to 1954.

During these years, the United States entered its own fatal involvement with Vietnam. In an effort to save Vietnam from becoming communist, the United States supplied the French forces with advisers and supplies. American aid quickly escalated, rising from approximately $150 million a year in 1950 to more than $1 billion in 1954. But Ho Chi Minh's forces proved far more difficult to defeat than expected. Finally, in 1954 the French lost the war, an event that led to the Geneva Accord, an agreement to temporarily divide Vietnam into two countries, North and South, along its seventeenth parallel. Elections to reunite the country, planned for later that year, were part of the agreement.

Fear of a communist victory in those elections sent nearly a million people fleeing from North Vietnam to the South. The communists had earned a reputation for ruthlessness during the French-Indochina War. Ho Chi Minh's Vietminh used harsh tactics, including kidnapping, jailing, and execution, against those citizens who opposed them. Civil liberties, including freedom of speech, had been severely curtailed. For these reasons, many Northerners, primarily the wealthy, deeply feared a communist takeover.

Political maneuvering and corruption throughout the country were widespread, however, and the promised elections were never held. Thus, the country was permanently divided into two nations: North Vietnam and South Vietnam.

A Country Divided

Vietnam was in conflict again. In the North, Ho Chi Minh pledged to heal the gash that had torn his country in two. He promised not only to reunite the two countries into one, but also to restore social justice. Ho Chi Minh vowed to destroy the age-old power of the wealthy landowners and give the farmers and peasants what they wanted most—their own land. At the same time, in the South, some Vietnamese began to strike out against their own weak leader, the American-supported Ngo Dinh Diem. Diem's favoritism toward his own family and his authoritarian rule made him

The French-Indochina War destroyed the countryside of Vietnam and left many of the people without food or shelter.

unpopular. In 1960 southern communists organized their own resistance forces, The National Liberation Front, better known as the Vietcong. A two-part civil war now raged: North versus South, and the Vietcong versus the Diem government.

Nguyen Tan Thanh, who served as a captain in the communist forces, described why he enlisted on that side.

In my village, there were about forty-three hundred people. Of these, maybe ten were landlords. . . . The rest of the people were tenants or poor honest farmers. I knew that the rich oppressed the poor. The poor had nothing to eat, and they also had no freedom. We had to get rid of the regime that allowed a few people to use their money and authority to oppress the others.[2]

This battle cry of social justice was an inspiration to the badly equipped communist army. The Soviet Union supported the North, but its own resources were meager. Inadequately equipped both in arms and in manpower, the northern forces relied on guerilla tactics—ambush, surprise raids, and sniper attacks.

For their part, the South Vietnamese forces were not only supplied with superior weaponry, but also with tens of thousands of American soldiers. Under the administration of President John F. Kennedy, the United States began sending troops to fight alongside the South Vietnamese. In 1963, 489 Americans were killed in Vietnam. Following Kennedy's assasination in November 1963, his successor, President Lyn-don B. Johnson, significantly stepped up American involvement in the war. According to figures released by the U.S. Department of Defense, the training and equipping of American forces, combined with support of the South Vietnamese efforts, ultimately cost the United States a total of more than $106 billion.

Life in a War Zone

By the mid 1960s, Vietnam was torn apart again. Some of the most advanced and powerful tools of modern warfare, supplied by both the United States and the Soviet Union, were aimed at the country. In an effort to uncover communist tunnels and hideouts, capitalist supporters sprayed millions of acres of jungle with defoliants. The

The fighting drove thousands of destitute Vietnamese to leave their homes and seek refuge in the cities.

lethal Agent Orange stripped the leaves off the trees and destroyed entire forests. Herbicides killed crops. Farming all but came to a halt, and the Vietnamese people began to starve. An economy built on fertile agricultural land was destroyed. During the war years, even rice, for centuries a Vietnamese staple, had to be imported to North Vietnam from California. Roads and railroad tracks were damaged beyond use. Bridges, wharves, and dams lay in ruins. The country's infrastructure was unstable. An American government official, later describing the war, said, "It was as if we were trying to build a house with a bulldozer and wrecking crane."[3]

For the Vietnamese, rocket (a projectile weapon) and howitzer (short cannons) attacks were daily occurrences. The U.S. Air Force flew countless sorties (missions) with B-52 strategic bombers, each of which was equipped to drop 37,000 pounds of bombs. In fact, more bombs were dropped during the Vietnam War than during World War II and the Korean War combined. Furthermore, so many land mines were set by both sides that walking in rural areas remained treacherous decades after the war ended. And, even though most of the fighting took place in the countryside, the capital cities of Hanoi in the North and Saigon in the South were also the scenes of bombings and sniper attacks.

The relentless violence deprived hundreds of thousands of Vietnamese of their homes and livelihoods. As the war progressed and the bombing attacks became increasingly frequent, more people abandoned their rural villages and sought refuge in the cities. Saigon's population in 1961 was three hundred thousand, but by 1975, it was more than 3 million. The populations of the cities Da Nang, Nha Trang, and Hue also swelled. Refugees poured into these areas with little more than the clothes on their backs.

A Country Divided

Vietnam has a history of division. Physically, the country is split into highlands and lowlands. Socially and economically, it was divided for centuries between the wealthy few and the peasant majority. One of Vietnam's traditional creation myths explains these divisions. The myth tells how many years ago, in the land now called Vietnam, the dragon lord Lac Long Quan married the beautiful fairy princess Au Co. At first they lived very happily, and had one hundred sons.

But over time, the two could not get along, and Lac Long Quan took fifty of their sons with him to live in the fertile green delta by the sea. Queen Au Co chose to take the other fifty sons to live with her in the pure mountain forests.

Legend holds that this is why the people of the highlands and lowlands have never gotten along, and why Vietnam has had such a long history of partition and unrest.

Saigon

Saigon became a symbol of the war's effect on Vietnam. The city had always been a Vietnamese center of culture and commerce. Under French influence, it had become almost more European than Asian, with its wide boulevards and city squares. A river port, Saigon was a prosperous city home to many of the elite refugees who fled from the North in 1954 after the end of the French-Indochina War.

During the early years of the Vietnam War, Saigon boomed. The South Vietnamese welcomed the Americans, not only because they hoped the Americans would win the war and defeat communism, but also because the Americans' free-spending ways were good for Saigon's economy. Yet as the war dragged on, Saigon's economy changed. Refugees from the countryside poured into the city, starving, often sick or wounded, and with no possessions beyond what they could carry. While the merchants of Saigon were raking in profits, the rest of the city population and the rest of the country were being destroyed.

Those who supported U.S. involvement, and had profited by it, still hoped that the South could win the war, even as evidence of its terrible toll became apparent. Duong Van Mai Elliott, a Vietnamese reporter who subsequently immigrated to the United States, lived in Saigon during the last days of the war. In her memoir *The Sacred Willow*, she recalled how the fighting damaged the already frayed fabric of Vietnamese life:

> At the top, life could not have been better for the corrupt officers and officials, for men and women working as clerks for the Americans. . . . It was also good for those catering to Americans' needs, from prostitutes . . . to tailors, to . . . taxi drivers taking free-spending G.I.s around town on their furloughs [days off]. . . . Side by side with this hedonism [pleasure seeking] was the sad evidence of a crumbling society. Thousands and thousands of peasants were flocking into Saigon to escape the fighting in their villages. . . . On the sidewalks, we could see maimed people dragging themselves and begging for money. Street urchins—orphaned or homeless children called "the dust of life"—pestered pedestrians, begging, stealing. . . . Garbage piled up in many parts of the city. Near my parents' home, a huge mound attracted swarms of flies and rats, as the slum behind their quarters swelled with more and more people. Destitute adults and children rummaged through it to find something they could salvage.[4]

The Longest War

As the war progressed and Vietnam deteriorated, American awareness of the conflict grew. During Johnson's presidency, the war became nightly news.

The expanding media coverage began to reveal terrible atrocities on both sides, and opposition to American involvement mounted. Hundreds of thousands of protesters marched on Washington, D.C., demanding the United States withdraw its forces. As brutal and as costly as the war

American planes sprayed the defoliant Agent Orange over the jungles of Vietnam.

was, many questioned whether the United States had any right to be there. The spiraling cost, coupled with the loss of so many young lives, led to 1966 Senate hearings on whether the national interest was being served. Was the communist threat really so huge? senators asked. Was winning the war worth thousands of American deaths?

Meanwhile, in Vietnam, the fighting continued. In 1968 the North Vietnamese launched the Tet Offensive, capturing cities across South Vietnam and damaging the American embassy in Saigon. In retaliation, the United States leveled entire villages in an effort to drive the Vietcong out of the

South. Explaining army tactics, an American officer said, "It became necessary to destroy the town in order to save it."[5]

By this time, the enormous cost of the war had damaged the American economy. The government was engaged in serious deficit spending in an effort to pay for both the war and its many other foreign commitments. Other countries had begun to lose confidence in the American economy. When American businesses began to protest the war as detrimental to their interests, pressure to withdraw troops increased.

By 1973 even those who continued to insist that U.S. involvement was moral and necessary were conceding that a clear-cut victory was unlikely. No matter how many troops or how much firepower the United States poured into the country, the communist forces continued to hold their ground. At home, opposition to the war had spread to both major political parties. Protests were rampant. Both foreign and domestic business interests urged an end to the massive expenditures. In response to mounting criticism, in 1973, President Richard Nixon began to withdraw U.S. troops and vowed to turn the war over to the South Vietnamese.

A Swift, Terrifying End

Without American support, the feeble South Vietnamese government could not sustain the war. The end came within two years. In the spring of 1975, South Vietnam's leaders gave the order not to defend the country's northern highlands. Surrendering this strategic border was tantamount to admitting defeat. The South Vietnamese army took to the roads in a massive, panicked retreat. A reporter for the *New York Times* described the country in those last chaotic days of the war, saying, "It was as though someone had tugged at the loose end of a giant skein of yarn. The whole thing just came unwound."[6]

About 1 million civilians joined the fleeing army, following mostly on foot. At times the column of families stretched as far as twenty miles. Ly Thi Tinh, the widow of a South Vietnamese soldier, and her five children were among those who fled. Of the retreat she said, "We didn't know what to do. . . . We picked up everything in bags and ran to the neighbor's home. Everyone was crying. . . . Every-

As the war neared its end refugees fled the advance of the communist forces, pouring into Saigon on foot and in overloaded vehicles.

The Fall of Saigon

The drama of Saigon's surrender to communist forces was front-page news. George Esper, a reporter for the New York Times, *vividly described in this article dated April 30, 1975, the desperation of the Vietnamese hoping to be evacuated:*

With American fighter planes flying over and marines standing guard on the ground, Americans left Saigon yesterday by helicopter after fighting off throngs of Vietnamese civilians who tried to go along.

Eighty-one helicopters from carriers in the South China Sea landed at Tan Son Nhut airport and on roofs at the United States Embassy compound to pick up most of the approximately 1,000 remaining Americans and several thousand Vietnamese.

But large groups of other Vietnamese clawed their way up the 10 foot wall of the embassy compound in desperate attempts to escape approaching Communist troops. . . . After the last marines had left, hundreds of civilians swarmed into the compound and onto the roof. On the roof of a nearby building that had also served as a helipad, several hundred civilians huddled together, hoping there would be more helicopters to take them away. . . . People held up their children, asking Americans to take them. . . . During the airport evacuation, two Vietcong rockets whistled overhead and exploded behind the United States defense attache's compound. . . . Four buses drove around Saigon, picking up American, European, and Vietnamese evacuees. As the first bus arrived at the gates of Tan Son Nhut Air Base, Vietnamese guards fired at it.

where there were bodies. I knew I would die."[7] Ly Thi Tinh eventually made it to Saigon, but not before two of her children died, and another was separated from her, never to be found.

Fear of the imminent communist victory united peasants like Ly Thi Tinh with citizens of the wealthy, upper classes. Both lived in uncertainty and fear. Many of the better educated, urban Vietnamese had already fled the communists once, in 1954 when the country was divided. They had firsthand experience of a communist takeover and did not want to repeat it.

Once again, more than twenty years later, they feared jail and torture; they dreaded the loss of freedom of religion and speech. A civil servant, whose brother had been executed by the communists twenty years earlier for aiding the French, described the pain he and his family had already suffered because of communist tactics:

My brother . . . was kidnapped and killed by the Viet Minh [northern communist soldiers]. . . . The Viet Minh lied to my family. They said that my brother still survived, but had to do some kind of mission for them. We found this out about a year after he had disappeared. The Viet Minh women came to my mother's house in her village. They asked my sister to help them with making cakes for the Viet Minh soldiers. In fact they were trying to detect whether she was sad or happy due to the fact that her eldest brother was missing. So they said, "Your eldest brother was arrested. Do you miss him? Do you love him?"

My sister realized that they would report what she said, so to survive she replied, "I don't care; I don't love him; I don't miss him. What he did, he has to suffer for it."

My mother had sad feelings inside just as did my sister. My mother loved her son, but outside she pretended.[8]

Many Vietnamese had heard such rumors and secondhand accounts of communist tactics. The stories terrified them, making the imminent takeover a nightmare. They expected an immediate and violent reprisal by the victors. This common belief was expressed by one resident who predicted, "The communists are about to win and they'll drench the South in a sea of blood."[9]

Throngs of Vietnamese people desperately scaled the wall of the U. S. Embassy in Saigon during the day and night of April 29, 1975. Only the lucky reached the evacuation helicopters and safety.

Vietnamese refugees were flown to the United States in the summer of 1975.

April 1975

As the communist forces marched toward Saigon, the U.S. government shared these fears. Its primary concern was for the lives of the thousands of American citizens still in Vietnam. Some were government advisers and officials employed by the American embassy. Others were military officials and personnel. Teachers, doctors, and employees of charitable organizations still worked there. In addition, business-people employed by American companies with Vietnamese offices were still working in Saigon and other cities.

By March 1975, the U.S. government, headed by President Gerald Ford, was secretly flying these American citizens, their dependents, and selected Vietnamese out of the country. These flights were meant to evacuate only Americans and Vietnamese with American connections, but they were in fact filled with anyone who could beg or barge aboard. The stampede to leave was on.

CHAPTER TWO

In Search of Safety

*Duong di kho khong kho vi ngan nui cach
   song,*

kho vi long nguoi ngai nui e song,

*The road is difficult not because it is
   blocked by a mountain or a river.*

*It is difficult because people are afraid of
   the river and the mountain.*

—Vietnamese poem. In Gail Paradise
Kelly, *From Vietnam to America*.

The communist takeover of Vietnam set off two waves of immigration to the United States. The first wave began in the spring of 1975 and continued

into 1977. The Vietnamese who left during these years were relatively well-educated and westernized. Some had contacts in the United States and were fortunate enough to be evacuated with the help of the American government. However, approximately fifty thousand more refugees who fled during this time left on their own initiative, escaping either on foot or in small boats.

The second wave of Vietnamese immigration began in 1978, and has lasted until today, peaking in 1980 when ninety-five thousand immigrants arrived in the United States. Those who left during the second wave were significantly poorer and less educated than earlier immigrants of the first wave. Between 1978 and the early 1980s, the escape route for these refugees was the South China Sea, via small, rickety boats. The journey of the immigrant was marked by severe hardship, often death, and it came to be a symbol not only of Vietnamese immigration, but also of the suffering of refugees around the world.

The First, Lucky Few

By late April 1975, communist artillery was slamming Saigon. Panic rocked the city. Vietnamese begging to be evacuated besieged the American embassy. With Saigon's airport closed because of shelling damage, the only routes out of the country were by boat or helicopter. The original American evacuation plan, an orderly airlift of eligible individuals to ships waiting offshore, proved woefully inadequate. In the last days before Saigon fell to the communists, getting out of Vietnam came to depend more on sheer luck than anything else.

Andrew X. Pham, a Vietnamese American writer, was a young boy living in Saigon with his family during the communist takeover. He described the atmosphere on the night of April 29, 1975:

In a desperate effort to survive, hundreds of thousands of Vietnamese fled their homeland with only the clothes on their backs.

The night was choked with those who fled, those who hid, those who scavenged. . . . Mom and Dad were busy packing suitcases and burning documents, so I was able to sneak out of the house. . . . I burst onto the street. Crashed into the flood of refugees swarming in one direction. Refuse covered the ground, stampeded over and over again. The air reeked of smoke, loud with people. Down the road, the fish market was burning unchecked. Gunfire snapped in staccato across the city. Somewhere far away a siren howled. . . . Growling helicopters skimmed low, their humping air vibrating my ribs, their rope ladders trailing behind like kite tails. . . . In the narrows, people crushed and hammered each other against brick walls, stampeding, barreling to salvation—the American ships waiting in the harbor.[10]

The State Department had formally committed to evacuating only American citizens, their dependents, and those Vietnamese currently or formerly employed by the U.S. government. However, many American administrators sympathized with anyone who had supported the United States. As a result, an untold number of people whose names did not appear on official evacuation lists also were able to leave.

During the week of April 21, more than five thousand people a day were airlifted out of Saigon's airport. Most were flown to American military vessels waiting offshore. One immigrant, who now lives with his family in Seattle, was among of them.

I left Vietnam by boat, and headed to Hong Kong. I was helped by Americans who gave me American money to buy my ticket so that I could more easily escape Saigon. . . . When I got to Hong Kong, I had an American sponsor which my [American] army

Refugees, Not Immigrants

The Vietnamese who came to the United States after the collapse of South Vietnam were not really immigrants. Immigrants leave their homeland voluntarily, with a destination in mind. The Vietnamese did not leave by choice, and most of them were unsure where they would end up. A more accurate word to describe them is refugee. In Hearts of Sorrow, *author James A. Freeman provides this United Nations definition of a refugee:*

[A refugee is] any person who, owing to a well-founded fear of being persecuted for reasons of race, religion, nationality, or political opinion, is outside the country of his nationality and is unable or, owing to such fear for reasons other than personal convenience, is unwilling to avail himself of the protection of that country; or . . . is unwilling to return to it.

The first Vietnamese to reach America were the professionals and military officers and their families.

friends had arranged for me. Since I already knew English, and since I had letters from my friends who were going back to live in the states, I did not have a hard time getting to America. I was very lucky.[11]

These very first refugees were professionals—doctors, dentists, lawyers—or military officers and their families. They stepped off the military airplanes wearing tailored suits and silk dresses, carrying patent leather suitcases. According to a U.S. Army doctor working at a refugee center, "They were the VIPs, the cream of the crop, all first class passengers."[12]

A Frightening Journey

Despite the rush to leave the country, the actual takeover of Saigon turned out to be relatively peaceful. The South Vietnamese put up no resistance, thereby averting a violent confrontation. Yet the stream of early refugees did not diminish. Instead, it continued to swell. From the end of April to the middle of May that year, approximately 132,000 people fled Vietnam. These refugees left not on American planes and ships but on their own initiative. Again, many were western educated. Northerners who had immigrated south in 1954, as well as elite Southerners, were all represented. Some were able to purchase exit permits, which were expensive due to rampant corruption of officials and because South Vietnam officially forbade anyone from leaving. Many more simply escaped.

Few anticipated the obstacles awaiting them. Many left by night, walking through the forests, carrying whatever they could. Food and water were scarce. Bandits were a constant threat. Stepping on unexploded mines was an almost daily experience. Many refugees went overland toward Thailand, only to be killed by Cambodian communist forces. The elderly and frail, along with infants in arms, all took part in these arduous, highly dangerous treks. A woman who eventually made it to the United States described the trauma of her family's escape this way:

I carried my daughter until I was exhausted, and then I asked my sister

Escape for Vietnamese peasants was a harrowing ordeal, with little to eat or drink and a constant fear of bandits.

for help. Every step made us afraid. I didn't know what to do. If we went back we would die, so we just kept going forward, hearing stories all of the time about others who had made it okay. We tried not to think about it a lot, but it was all around us, and we couldn't get it out of our heads.[13]

The thousands who fled left neighbors and friends behind. Some people who stayed did not want to abandon their homeland. Others couldn't find a means of escape. Still others, now that the war was finally over, hoped to contribute to rebuilding their country. The communist regime promised a new era of economic prosperity and social justice. This, however, proved a most difficult promise to fulfill.

Life Under Communism

The communists inherited a devastated, divided nation. Much of the land, ravaged by bombing and chemical warfare, could not be farmed. The country's infrastructure was all but destroyed, making transport of food and goods difficult. Thousands of rural villagers with no means of supporting themselves had crowded into the cities. Hospitals were low on supplies; medical needs could not always be met. The new government's task was enormous, and its efforts proved unsuccessful.

Communism is based on the economic theory that property should be equally distributed, and that, rather than support upper and lower classes, a society should be classless. Moving swiftly to convert the entire country to communism, the new Vietnamese government put an end to free enterprise. Initially it targeted the most wealthy, the symbols of the old regime. Demonstrating their complete authority, the communists punished those who had profited from capitalism. For example, a successful businessman who had supplied the South Vietnamese Army with barbed wire was arrested and sentenced to twenty years in jail.

Next, in a campaign begun in 1978, the government seized all small businesses, claiming their goods and assets for the state. Shops were shut down or taken over by the government. Thirty thousand private businesses were nationalized. The owners of these properties were forced to leave their homes and relocate to rural areas, termed New Economic Zones. This government initiative moved people out of the overcrowded cities and back into the abandoned countryside. Relocated to remote areas, including the highlands, families were given a piece of land, a hut, and a rice subsidy to tide them over until they could begin to raise their own crops.

This government policy created mass panic among the people of Vietnam. Many merchants, whose businesses were seized, chose to flee. At the same time, the farmers were distressed over the government's takeover of food production and distribution. This new policy forced peasants to join farming cooperatives, and to sell their surplus crops to the government at government-established prices. In protest, farmers in the South, accustomed to independent enterprise, burned their crops or fed them to pigs, rather than supply the state. The government also began a system of food rationing, which allowed its officials tight control over families and villages. A series of poor harvest years contributed to the people's misery. Malnutrition became widespread, and in desperation, some people ate grain usually fed only to horses.

Yet another factor in the steadily deteriorating standard of living was the U.S. embargo on trade, which had been in effect against North Vietnam since 1964 and was extended to the whole country in 1975.

Twenty-Five Years of Fear and Hope

The story of the boat people did not end in the 1980s. A steady stream of Vietnamese continued to leave into the late 1990s. By that time, repression in Vietnam had lessened, and these immigrants were largely fleeing poverty. In the article, "Vietnam's Boat People: 25 Years of Fears, Hopes, and Dreams," Scott McKenzie, a reporter for CNN.com, describes how, over the twenty-five years since the first boat people left, the world changed its mind about how to treat them.

By the late 1980s, . . . the ports of first asylum in Asia and the resettlement countries were reconsidering their policies. Resettlement ratios had flip-flopped: arrivals outweighed departures. A new breed of boat people was taking to the seas. They were, for the most part, economic refugees. . . .

It was at this point the international community, in tandem with the U.N. High Commissioner for Refugees, met to produce what was termed the Comprehensive Plan of Action. The plan agreed upon in 1989 did two key things. The first was to ensure all arrivals in

ports of first asylum continued to be screened, or "tested", to determine whether they were genuine refugees, according to U.N. convention, or economic migrants. The second element of the plan was a return program for those who failed the refugee "test". . . .

For the first time Vietnamese boat people were being repatriated [sent back home] en masse. . . . Hong Kong, where tens of thousands of boat people had run aground, encountered the worst circumstances. . . . Protests in the camps became commonplace. . . . [But] the taxpayers of Hong Kong were fed up [with] paying to house Vietnamese boat people and were prepared to allow brute force to be used. . . . Even the United States agreed the only option was repatriation, voluntary or otherwise.

A small team of dedicated lawyers pushed for the rights of individuals such as [Vietnamese refugee] Ngo Van Ha. He was an orphan whose relatives in Vietnam had refused to take him back. . . . When he won the right to join relatives in the United States there was celebration in the camps.

This prohibition against all trade meant that the United States and its allies withheld any assistance from Vietnam. Most war-torn countries, though, require help from other nations to rebuild. Such help was not available to the newly communist Vietnam.

Vietnamese writer Duong Van Mai Elliott summarized this situation:

> The heavy-handed state control that clamped down over the economy brought disastrous results. With peace, the standard of living declined, rather than rose. Shortages became serious. Part of the problem was the embargo that the United States had imposed. . . . When all of America's friends followed its lead, Vietnam became isolated. . . . Even with international help, it would have been difficult to get the country back on its feet. Without it, the task became herculean [very difficult].[14]

Reeducation and Religious Persecution

The lack of international support simply encouraged the communists, rather than undermining them as intended. The new regime was totalitarian, meaning that it aimed to exert complete control over the lives of its citizens. Dissent or rebellion became almost impossible. Scott C. S. Stone and John E. McGowan, authors of *Wrapped in the Wind's Shawl*, interviewed a man who had fled Vietnam and was waiting, along with his four children, to be transferred out of a refugee camp. He described how political conditions, primarily the loss of free speech, had grown intolerable for him:

> First you must understand why we left. It was not just the economic conditions, bad as they were. It was because we had no freedom of speech and we had to lie all the time. We had not much freedom of anything, but mostly I got tired of having to lie. If we were asked by the government if we had enough food we had to say yes, even though we had little food. If we said no, there was not enough to eat, there would be some form of punishment. . . . If they offer you food, you must say no, you are not hungry.[15]

The communists' most extreme method of quashing resistance, though, was to round up southern officials and sympathizers and imprison them in reeducation camps. Told to pack their belongings for a stay of ten days to two weeks, many did not return for years. Thousands of professionals, including doctors, engineers, and teachers from the South, were isolated and intimidated in these camps. Conditions were harsh. Malnutrition, denial of medical care, and physical and psychological abuse were common. Some prisoners died from extreme conditions or were executed. Others escaped, only to be recaptured.

The camps were the most frightening, but not the only, form of repression. Religious gatherings were frequently disrupted or prevented. Buddhist-run orphanages were taken over by the state. Buddhist teachers who refused to teach communist doctrine were arrested. A

Buddhist nun who left in 1978 remembers, "They encourage sons to denounce fathers, students to accuse teachers, and novices to betray their monks. This is very difficult. . . . After three years of living under Communist rule, I realized that they intended to destroy religion."[16]

Hopes for social justice under communism, then, were dashed. The country so many Vietnamese had loved, and where they had been happy, no longer existed. A Vietnamese American who fled at the age of seventeen while still a high school student, lived under communism for four years. Reflecting on the experience, he commented, "After 1975 the people in Vietnam hated the Communists. Some of them supported the Communists and gave them food and rice during their fight against the South Vietnamese government. Now they regret it. They realize that it was like feeding a lion cub who, when it grows up, eats those who fed it."[17]

Return to War

Compounding the suffering of many Vietnamese was a new war begun in 1978, this time with neighboring Cambodia. Cambodia's government, the repressive Khmer Rouge, had begun shelling Vietnamese villages and killing peasants. In 1978 the Vietnamese army invaded Cambodia and succeeded in taking over the capital city. However, continued Khmer Rouge resistance kept the Vietnamese engaged in war

These refugees, crammed onto a small boat and standing in the pouring rain, were rescued on the open sea.

Proud to Be Poor

Lan Nguyen grew up in North Vietnam after the war ended. Although many Vietnamese found the desperate poverty of those years a reason to flee, her family, which identified itself as communist, had a different perspective. In the article, "Wartime Ghosts Haunt Vietnamese-U.S. Relations," Carol Clarke, a reporter for CNN.com, interviewed Nguyen about those postwar years, and how her anti-American views slowly changed.

Her parents, both teachers, had to work second jobs to survive. Lan and her older sister also worked at home after school, stitching cloth for a textile company. Food was scarce and of poor quality.

Poverty was not something to escape. It was as natural as the weather to Lan and her young friends. "We just thought communists were poor," she said. "We were proud to be poor. If someone said, 'My family is poor,' you would say, 'My family is poorer.'"

When she reached high school, however, information began trickling in about another way of life.

"We started hearing about America, that it was a very rich country, very different from what it was like in Vietnam," she said. "Our books said that America was all bad, and the rumors said it was all good. We were very curious. Everyone wanted to go there, to know what it was really like."

for the next ten years. A new military draft was instituted, and the nation's few resources were being funneled to the army. Vietnam's per capita income sank to the second lowest in the world.

In 1979 Vietnam was invaded again, this time by China, Cambodia's ally. The Chinese were quickly defeated, but not before their soldiers had done heavy damage to villages along the Chinese Vietnamese border.

The Ethnic Chinese

China's invasion was responsible for the immigration of a large and influential group of Vietnamese, the ethnic Chinese. Having left southern China at the turn of the century, the Chinese Vietnamese people had never been welcomed in Vietnam. Under the French, they had received special treatment and prospered as bankers, lenders, merchants, and tradespeople. Now, under communism, their businesses were confiscated, and they were targeted as enemies of the state. After the 1979 invasion by China, already hostile attitudes toward the ethnic Chinese became outright persecution. Their schools were shut down, and a curfew specifically targeting the Chinese was imposed.

As a result, ethnic Chinese made up a large portion of those who sought asylum in the United States during the second wave of immigration. The Vietnamese government officially allowed Chinese to leave, provided they could pay the appropriate fees. Thousands left between the years 1978 and 1981. Those who could not afford to buy their way out joined the tens of thousands of other Vietnamese who escaped during these years, the group that came to be known as the "boat people."

The Boat People

Within three years after the fall of Saigon, the South China Sea became a stage for a desperate drama watched by much of the world. The media spotlight shone on thousands of refugees fleeing in rickety boats.

These Vietnamese could not have chosen a more dangerous escape route. Soldiers closely guarded Vietnam's shores, so simply boarding a boat required the utmost subterfuge. Some people bribed government workers for passage onto a vessel; families paid up to $2,000 apiece for their voyage. Others bartered with boat owners, trading food or family treasures; many had no choice but to turn over whatever valuables they had, ensuring they would start their new lives in poverty. Frequently, families pooled their resources to purchase passage out for one or two members, in the hopes that once they reached America, they would be able to send for those left behind.

Another reason this escape was so dangerous was that neither the tiny Viet-

namese fishing boats nor the other small craft—sampans—were meant for rough, open seas. Many sampans were in pitiful shape; they leaked and had unreliable engines. Monsoons and overcrowded conditions also made sinking a constant danger. Pirates roamed both the South China Sea and the Gulf of Thailand (another escape route) and frequently attacked the frail boats; passengers were robbed, raped, murdered. Starvation and exposure to the sun claimed the lives of the very young and very old.

Packed so closely there was often no room for anyone to sit, let alone lie, down, the refugees pinned their hopes on a quick rescue that did not materialize. Instead, their days onboard frequently stretched into weeks. Boats ran out of fuel. Many were not equipped with compasses, so they lost direction and drifted. Meager supplies of food and water were quickly depleted. Politeness and respect, so important to Vietnamese society, gave way to desperation and fear.

Because there is no way of knowing exactly how many Vietnamese escaped this way, there is no way of knowing the exact numbers who died. Some historians estimate that as many as 50 percent of boats suffered casualties. Author Duong Van Mai Elliot tells the story of one immigrant, a young man named Nam, who escaped Vietnam in one of these boats:

The night before [Nam and his family left Vietnam], they had endured a nerve-wracking vigil, waiting for three hours in the dark for the tide to rise [so their boat could leave]. At eleven o'clock, they finally lifted anchor and sailed into the stormy night. Swells made many of the passengers violently sick. . . . During the day, the refugees would bake in the hot sun; as darkness fell and the fog descended, they would freeze. . . . Nam would sneak up and sleep next to the engine to keep warm. There was no privacy onboard. . . .

One night, Nam thought he heard voices rising over the water. The sound was eerie, like hundreds of people whispering in the fog, and he felt a chill going down his spine. The next day, the captain said that they had just sailed past an area of the ocean where perhaps thousands of refugees had perished. Later, one of Nam's brothers would disappear into the ocean without a trace. Sometimes Nam wonders whether his brother has joined that chorus of ghosts over that patch of the sea.[18]

Seeking Asylum

Many boats tried to put ashore in neighboring countries, but were turned away by government officials. Most countries bordering Vietnam had their own political and economic troubles. Thus, Thailand, Malaysia, the Republic of Indonesia, Hong Kong, and the Philippines were the nearest points of safety for the refugees, but none of these countries intended to be a place of asylum. In fact, all these nations were reluctant to take on the burden of thousands of refugees in dire need of food, shelter, and medical care.

Initially, the governments of Thailand and Malaysia helped, but the numbers of Vietnamese quickly became overwhelming. As the exodus went on, far longer and in far greater numbers than predicted, these countries found it very difficult to offer asylum. By 1979 Malaysia refused to accept any more refugees. As Thailand's ef-

Powerful Protest

The actions of communist leaders in the Socialist Republic of Vietnam (the country's official name) distressed not only Vietnamese, but also observers around the world. A group of prominent Americans who had opposed the Vietnam War wrote an open letter to Vietnam's president, condemning the country's repressive tactics. Because the letter writers had once been extremely critical of outside involvement in Vietnam, their criticism of the communists was unexpected and powerful. The following is an exerpt of the letter, as reprinted in E. B. Fincher's book The Vietnam War:

With tragic irony, the cruelty, violence and oppression practiced by foreign powers in your country for more than a century continue today under the present regime. Thousands of innocent Vietnamese, many whose only "crime" are those of conscience, are being arrested, detained, and tortured in prisons and re-education camps. People disappear and never return. For many, life is hell and death is prayed for.

forts also flagged, Indonesia temporarily accepted Vietnamese refugees, but only in small numbers. Even comparatively wealthy nations such as Japan, Hong Kong, and Singapore were leery of jeopardizing their resources by taking on the crushing burden of so many people in such great need.

Making the situation even more critical, another nearby refugee crisis developed—this time in Cambodia. The Cambodian government toppled and was replaced by a violent, repressive dictatorship. As a result, thousands of Cambodians began to flee and headed overland for Thailand. As Vietnam became embroiled in its own war with Cambodia, the number of refugees increased even further, placing yet a heavier strain on the Thai government. The situation culminated in Thailand's refusing eighty thousand refugees in 1979, even though their return to Cambodia was an almost certain death sentence.

As a result, the Vietnamese refugees whose boats weathered the dangers of the seas and actually made it within sight of shore were frequently not allowed to land. Met by guns and threats, many were forced to return to the open sea. Some refugees purposely sank their boats within sight of shore, in the hopes that authorities would let them land rather than drown.

Rescue

In this desperate situation, rescue ultimately came in many forms. Some boats were welcomed to the shores of Malaysia or the Philippines. Others were picked up by Malaysian or Thai fishermen, or by shipping vessels or oil tankers from European countries. A young refugee named Pham, who cannot say how long or where his boat drifted, remembers the moment he spotted a large ship in the distance. Too weak from hunger and exhaustion to identify it, he feared it was one of the dreaded communist patrol boats, which frequently recaptured the refugee vessels. He said, "My eyes were hurting from the salt and I could not see the ship very well. People in front of me were crying, and I heard a woman say it was an American ship. I could not see for myself, and I just prayed that she was right."[19]

Pham and his fellow passengers were picked up by a U.S. Navy vessel and turned over to refugee officials of the United Nations. Eventually, Pham made it to America, where he lives today.

The Asian Refugee Camps

Even after being picked up by Asian, European, or American ships, the refugees in this second wave had only reached their first stop. Upon arrival they were transferred to at least one, and sometimes a series, of refugee camps.

The camps in Thailand, Malaysia, the Republic of Indonesia, Singapore, and Hong Kong were called first asylum camps. The camps were established through negotiations with the United Nations High Commissioner for Refugees; the American Red Cross assisted. These camps were for those refugees who had minimal or no contacts in the United States. They were holding centers for people whose future placement was un-

A Vietnamese "boat" woman uses a blanket to shelter herself and her child from the blazing sun.

certain. Focusing on physical survival, the first asylum camps provided little more than the bare necessities. Here, refugees waited weeks, months, sometimes even years, to be permanently transferred to the United States. Vietnamese American writer Hien Duc Do, who fled Saigon with his family in April, 1975, describes how refugees coped as they waited in the first camps.

Southeast Asian refugee camps . . . were primarily located in areas away from the indigenous population. The degree of . . . freedom in each camp varied according to the country and the local authorities. Input from the refugees themselves ranged from none—where conditions were prison-like—to some—where conditions were more open. . . .

Since these camps were thought to have been temporary, most structures were hastily constructed. Refugees were allocated small, limited living spaces. Often, three to four tiers of bunk beds were added to accommodate entire families. . . . Food was directly distributed and rationed by camp authorities, or food was prepared in communal kitchens and eaten in dining halls. In some cases, in order to supplement their diets, refugees cultivated small plots of land. . . . Wherever they were allowed, refugees worked as manual laborers for the local communities. In some camps, small shops and businesses were established and run by the refugees.[20]

Buddhist monks and nuns fled their homeland when the communists made practicing their religion difficult.

The better camps also provided basic language and vocational classes.

Life in the transitional camps, whether during the first or second wave, was just a continuation of the immigrants' long and difficult journey. They fled war, poverty, political oppression, and a ravaged nation that could no longer support its population. Thus, enduring both emotional and physical hardship, searching for a safe place, they set out on another voyage, crossing the Pacific Ocean for America without knowing what lay ahead.

CHAPTER THREE

Welcome to Freedom Land

When the refugees arrived [in the United States], they landed with a clean slate and started from scratch. Their material possessions were virtually identical: little more than the clothes on their backs. Thus, when we speak of what they brought with them, the referent is not their material possessions but their cultural heritage.

—Nathan Caplan, John K. Whitmore, and Marcella H. Choy, *The Boat People.*

Permanent resettlement was a long and complex process. Escape was only the beginning. Those who left in the first wave spent a brief time in Asian refugee camps before being transferred to one of four transitional camps hastily set up in the United States. After these transitional camps, their next step was to find an American sponsor who would help them with the huge tasks of finding work and housing.

For those who came in the second wave, the transition was even more difficult. Because the American camps were closed in 1976, these later immigrants skipped the transitional camps and were swept directly from their Asian camp experience into a new, alien culture.

Their journeys turned out to be far more treacherous than imagined. Confused, fearful about starting over, and grieving for their abandoned homeland, many clung to the promise of a new life in the United States—or Freedom Land, as some refugees dubbed it—as their only solid hope.

Why the United States?

The United States had numerous reasons for accepting Vietnamese immigrants. By 1975, American Vietnamese ties went back more than a decade. The American government and, in large part, the American public, acknowledged a moral responsibility to a people who had lost everything in a war fought alongside American troops.

Adding to this feeling of responsibility was the long-standing tradition of aiding those who turned to the United States for rescue and freedom. In a 1975 speech urging Congress to appropriate money for aid to the Vietnamese, House Judiciary Chairman Peter Rodino declared, "When this country forgets its immigrant heritage and turns its back on the oppressed and homeless, we will indeed have written finis [the end] to the American dream."[21]

Two Vietnamese girls in a refugee camp peer through the barbed wire fence.

At Camp Pendleton, California, volunteers tried to make the children comfortable in their new culture.

Furthermore, by 1975, most Vietnamese had some familiarity with American culture. They had met American soldiers. Many had worked with American businesspeople. They had been exposed to American magazines, newspapers, and radio. The glimpses they had had of life in the United States looked enviably glamorous and wealthy. A South Vietnamese schoolteacher who left soon after the fall of

Saigon recalled her first impression on reaching her new country. "I was happy! America! It is just like heaven! Because people live here in freedom! You can go anywhere. You can live richer."[22]

American Camps Overseas

As a result of the responsibility Americans felt toward the Vietnamese, in April 1975 the U.S. government set up processing centers for those immigrants. These centers, or camps, served those immigrants deemed refugees—that is, people in need of political asylum, who were guaranteed entry into the United States. One of these camps was in the Philippines. Another, one of the largest and most well known, was located on the island of Guam, an American territory. Here Anderson Air Force Base, a facility abandoned since World War II, was hastily converted to temporary housing.

Within days of the first arrivals, officials on Guam realized that far more Vietnamese than anticipated would need accommodation. A makeshift "tent city" was created. Here the weary refugees received medical care, clothing, and any other necessities they lacked. Some were reunited with family. Others tried to get information about family members from whom they had been separated.

The journey and plight of these first refugees was front-page news in the American media. *Time* magazine described the center at Guam:

> The mammoth refugee complex bulges with 40,000 people. . . . At night, strands of arc lights create hard patches of brightness among the heavy canvas tents. The refugees leave urgent personal messages about themselves in graffiti all around the camp—on the fences leading into the huts and immigration tents, on the sides of the shower stalls, even in spray paint across their tent flaps. Said one sign, 'TRAN THI HONG DA DI CALIFORNIA.' (TRAN THI HONG GONE TO CALIFORNIA.)[23]

Tran Thi Hong was lucky. Many refugees spent a long time waiting in camps. Without connections, the necessary paperwork to go to America could drag on for months. In fact, the average refugee stay in a camp in Guam or the Philippines was nine months. After that, the immigrants were transferred to camps in the continental United States.

The American Camps

In the weeks after the fall of Saigon, the United States opened four transitional refugee camps on American soil. The first and largest was Camp Pendleton in southern California. The other three were Fort Chafee in Arkansas, Eglin Air Force Base in Florida, and Indiantown Gap in Pennsylvania. The camps were jointly run by the military, the government's Interagency Task Force on Indochina Refugees, and a wide range of volunteer organizations, which became known by the acronym Volags (Volunteer agencies). The Volags included among others the International Refugee Service, the YMCA, the Red Cross, and many church groups, among them the United Hebrew Immigrant Assistance Service, the Lutheran Immigration Service, and the U.S. Catholic Conference.

Upon arrival in the American camps, immigrants were interviewed and screened for security purposes, a daunting task for the officials involved. Julia Vadala Taft, who headed the Interagency Task Force, describes some of the obstacles.

> We had . . . to do security clearance [a background check to make sure the refugees were not a threat to American society]—we have a requirement

in this country that if you are being brought in or are allowed to come in, either as a parolee or a refugee, you have to get your security clearances. Well, come to find out that there were a lot of agencies involved in security clearances. . . . We [the Interagency Task Force] were finding that we weren't able to process people out of the camps for two or three weeks because the security clearance process was just a nightmare.[24]

Technicalities like this were common, and life in the American camps required a good deal of patience. Much of the immigrant's day was spent waiting in lines: for meals, for medical exams, for various forms of government processing, and for testing job skills and the English language comprehension. Translators helped determine hometowns, age, and the makeup of large family groups. In addition, the immigrants were fingerprinted by the Immigration and Naturalization Service and issued Social Security cards. During this time, families and individuals lived in large barracks or tents, which afforded little privacy. Still, adults and children alike were encouraged to attend classes, where they were instructed in English and introduced to American customs, and the plentiful food and clean water were a great improvement over the poorer conditions of most of the Asian camps.

A Vietnamese family learns the game of dominoes with their American sponsor family.

Yet many immigrants, describing their experience in the transitional camp, reported feeling discontent with their idleness and were uneasy about taking assistance from the government. Although little work was expected of them, many were eager to contribute, volunteering as translators, typists, or even cooks. At Camp Pendleton, dubbed "Operation New Arrival," the food served by military chefs—hamburgers, hot dogs, and spaghetti— caused stomach ailments among the newcomers. The Americans tried to oblige the immigrants' tastes, but in at least one case, they needed help. A *Time* magazine reporter wrote, "The Army had been supplying soggily cooked rice, but finally asked for help in its kitchens. Said a mess sergeant, 'Come and show me how to cook it properly.' A score of Vietnamese women volunteered."[25]

Adapting to their unfamiliar environment took place not only in the mess halls, but also in the immigrants' daily contact with the American lifestyle. Entertainment, for example, was plentiful. The immigrants played volleyball, soccer, and Ping Pong. Camp officials showed American movies and sponsored concerts of American music. For the children, watching television was a fascinating way to learn about their new culture. In addition, many younger refugees spent their free time with officials and with volunteers, getting to know their adopted country on a one-on-one basis.

The camps' mission was to help those who qualified make the transition from temporary refugee to immigrant. Once the Vietnamese had received their security clearance, refugees had four main routes to leaving the camps: repatriating to another country, returning to Vietnam, proving they

Help Wanted

Finding a sponsor was the ticket out of the American transitional camps for most Vietnamese. Would-be sponsors from around the country advertised in the camps' newspapers, offering the immigrants housing and employment. In From Vietnam to America, *author Gail Paradise Kelly provided examples of some sponsors' want ads.*

Two or three mechanics, one of whom should speak some English. The sponsor is a Datsun car dealer in Georgia. The position offers free housing, assistance with food and regular salary.

Two machinists, one of whom should speak English, for a position in Pennsylvania. Free housing and food. Starting wage at $2.10 per hour. If good performance, can increase to $4.00 per hour.

Family up to 8 people to go to Springfield, Oregon. Sponsor would train refugees to work in his hairdressing salons. Also jobs available as fruit pickers.

Two fishermen needed for job in Florida. Position pays $2.10 per hour with sponsorship. Housing to be provided in new house trailer plus farm animals and garden.

were self-sufficient, and finding an American sponsor. Sponsorship, ultimately became the route most Vietnamese took.

Sponsorship

Sponsoring an immigrant family was a substantial undertaking. American volunteer sponsors pledged to provide food, clothing, and shelter until the family became self-supporting. In addition, sponsors agreed to help the adults find work, to enroll the children in school, and to be available in any way to assist adaptation to American daily life. Although the government gave limited financial assistance, most of the responsibility fell on the sponsor. Andrew X. Pham was ten years old when his family fled Vietnam. He describes what sponsorship meant to him and his family:

> The First Baptist church of Shreveport, Louisiana was our bridge to America. They loaned us the airfares. They rented us one of the church properties, found Dad work, and generally took care of the family, making sure our transition to America was comfortable. . . . [At Christmas they gave us] our very first turkey . . . for our holiday feast. Mom said it was the biggest and funniest-looking chicken she had ever seen. Everything in America is big, she said, marveling.[26]

The job of the sponsors was made more challenging by the 1975 U.S. economic recession. Many Americans were feeling a financial strain and had little extra to spare. As a result, most sponsors were not individuals but groups. Some corporations that had previously employed the immigrants in Vietnam, including Pan Am, Bank of America, and the *New York Times*, offered to hire them at American offices. Other companies, eager to employ cheap labor, also became sponsors. A consortium of Volags also took on the task of matching refugees and sponsors. These volunteer agencies were assisted by a network of church groups. Local congregations from all across the country agreed to sponsor families.

An elderly woman from rural South Vietnam who immigrated with her family in 1975 was sponsored by a church. She recalls,

> Our sponsor rented us a two-bedroom townhouse. . . . Because a church member owned it, the rent was low. . . . The church provided everything for us: pots, bowls, dishes, a small washing machine . . . all of our needs were met. . . . The minister of the church and his son also helped us move and showed me how to use appliances that were new to me, such as the washing machine and the electric stove. The market was close by, so my husband would ride there on his bicycle and bring back food. Around noon, I would go to my sponsor's house to work on the garden we had started. . . . My sponsor bought us a gas lawn mower, and this enabled my youngest son to cut grass to earn money while attending school. . . . We are strange to them, but they helped us. That's very nice; that's precious.[27]

The Legacy of the Camps

The transitional camps had taken on an enormous task. At Camp Pendleton alone, more than 7 million meals were served, and 165 babies were born. Yet the chief focus of the camps had always been to move the Vietnamese out as quickly and as efficiently as possible. Julia Vadala Taft, director of the Interagency Task Force on Indochina Refugees, wanted all the camps to be closed by Christmas. In an interview published in a 1996 issue of *Vietnam* magazine, she remembered, "I wanted these people [the immigrants] to celebrate their very first American Christmas in their own homes. . . . That was the goal. We let the voluntary agencies know that this was something we wanted, and so we kept the pressure on them to speed up the processing."[28] Taft's goal became reality. By December 20, 1975, all four camps had closed.

Although the camps were helpful in many ways, the brief period they operated limited what they could do. Those Vietnamese who spoke English and had the most marketable job skills, were the most

Wanted: One Family

In contrast to potential employers, who emphasized skills, sponsoring churches specified the number of refugees they could support. In From Vietnam to America, *Gail Paradise Kelly reprints some ads that appeared in one transitional camp's newspaper.*

The following sponsorships are available at Church World Service...

1) Ellington, Connecticut	5 to 7 people
2) Mt. Joy, Pennsylvania	Family of 4
3) Altoona, Pennsylvania	7 to 8 people
4) Hatboro, Pennsylvania	4 to 6 people
5) Chewsville, Maryland	8 to 10 people

First Baptist Church, Holyoke, Massachusetts, will take two families up to 6 persons each.

New Castle First Methodist Church wants any type of family interested in living in New Castle, Pennsylvania.

easily placed with sponsors and left first. For the fishermen, farmers, and soldiers, as well as for those immigrants who spoke no English, finding a sponsor was more difficult. Furthermore, part of the government's resettlement strategy was to disperse the refugees all across the country, so no one geographic area would be saturated. Many Vietnamese, though, were reluctant to be sent places where they might be the only foreigners. Others were wary of being sponsored by churches other than their own religion. As months passed, pressure to close the camps forced some immigrants to accept sponsorships they would not have chosen on their own.

VIETNAMESE COMMUNITIES IN CALIFORNIA

Yolo County
Sacramento County
Oakland County
San Francisco County
San Jose Metropolitan Area
Riverside County
Los Angeles County
Orange County
San Diego County

To test a caption in the Immigrants in America series, include the phrase A quick brown fox jumps over the

Despite these limitations, the four American camps did fulfill their mission of helping the Vietnamese make the transition from temporary refugee to permanent immigrant. Beginning in 1976, however, arriving Vietnamese no longer had this stepping stone. Instead, they plunged directly into American society.

The Next Waves: 1976 to 1982

The camps' closing was supposed to be the end of U.S. resettlement efforts. The American government hoped that the exodus from Vietnam was over, and that the aid program would be completed by 1977.

However, the end of the Vietnam War by no means meant the end of the departures. Boat people continued to arrive in Malaysia, Thailand, Indonesia, the Philippines, and Singapore, where they crowded into camps overseen by the United Nations. By 1979 these Asian countries were experiencing what some scholars call "compassion fatigue." The countries' limited resources were strained by the destitute who continued to arrive with no end in sight, and their citizens, many of whom were in need themselves, protested, saying the Vietnamese were not their problem. Furthermore, despite humanitarian efforts, conditions in most of the camps were woefully inadequate, and the wait to leave was very long.

One young Vietnamese man described his experience in Thai refugee camps.

Khao I Dang, a refugee camp in Thai territory, was . . . crowded with more than a hundred thousand people living in terrible conditions with minimal food, medical services and shelter and no recreational or educational activities. . . . After eight months living in Khao I Dang, I was transferred to Chan Vu Ri camp [also in Thailand] to be interviewed for resettlement. Then came the day they announced the decision. Some were eligible to go directly to the United States because they had relatives there. The rest would be transferred again. . . . I was in the latter group.[29]

Red Tape

One reason for the seemingly endless wait was American immigration law. As of 1977 only three hundred Asian immigrants per month were allowed to enter the United

The Homecoming Act of 1988 made it possible for these Amerasian children and their mothers to relocate in America.

States. That same year, though, the U.S. Immigration Service decided to admit Vietnamese under seventh preference visas—visas applied to people who were escaping communism, thus allowing a person to enter the United States for two years. After two years, the refugee was required to seek immigrant status, and, eventually, permanent residence.

The Vietnamese took advantage of this opportunity, and by 1979 the numbers of refugees continued to grow. That year, the desperate plight of the boat people reached such proportions that the United States once again sent rescue ships to the South China Sea. World outcry against the immigrants' suffering pressured the Vietnamese government to agree to participate in the Orderly Departure Program, established under the jurisdiction of the United Nations High Commissioner for Refugees. This program enabled people to leave Vietnam legally, either to be reunited with family members or for other humanitarian reasons. Since 1979 more than 480,000 Vietnamese have legally entered the United States under the Orderly Departure Program.

In addition, in 1980 President Jimmy Carter pushed for the passage of the Refugee Act, a law aimed at reducing entry restrictions for the Vietnamese. This act created the Office of Refugee Resettlement, which administers programs and services for refugees within the United States. It also provided states with money to assist the new arrivals for thirty-six months, provided the states had a satisfactory plan for administering that assistance. This new legislation eased the way for tens of thousands more Vietnamese to come to America

A Hesitant Welcome

Arrival in America was bittersweet. Forced to leave, unable to bring many possessions, the immigrants felt a mixture of joy and fear. For most, the questions they faced were challenging: Where would they live?

Core Values

Social researcher Nathan Caplan, Asian expert John K. Whitmore, and therapist Marcella H. Choy conducted a comprehensive study of the hundreds of thousands of immigrants who left Vietnam, Cambodia, and Laos for the United States. In their interviews, reported in their book The Boat People, *they asked the immigrants to rate the values important to them. The researchers report,*

We . . . had the respondents indicate which three of these values they considered most important. The following, "core" values constitute the bedrock of the refugees' culturally derived beliefs.

• Education and Achievement

• A Cohesive Family

• Hard Work

Interestingly, the two values that the refugees called not at all important were "Fun and Excitement" and "Material Possessions."

How would they live? What did this new, alien country offer—and what would it ask of them?

If the Vietnamese were unclear about what to expect, so, too, were most Americans. The Vietnamese comprised the largest single refugee group ever to arrive in the United States within such a short span of time. Concern about their impact was widespread. A May 1975 nationwide Gallup Poll asked Americans whether evacuated South Vietnamese should be allowed to live in the United States. The majority of the respondants, 54 percent, said that they should not.

This opposition had many roots. For some Americans, involvement in Vietnam had been such a long, painful, ultimately humiliating experience that they wished to forget it. For others, bitter feelings against the "enemy" lingered, made all the stronger by ignorance about Vietnamese culture. The Buddhist religion, for example, was uncommon in the United States, and the Vietnamese language was a barrier. The Vietnamese were also seen as a potential drain on states' public assistance programs.

The greatest opposition, however, was the result of America's economic climate. In 1975 the United States had sunk into its worst recession in decades. Businesses shut down and many people lost their jobs; in 1975, almost 8 million Americans were unemployed. A growing imbalance of goods imported from Asia angered some citizens, who blamed foreigners for putting Americans out of work. With jobs at a premium, many Americans opposed allowing foreigners in to compete for those jobs. This resentment was generalized toward Vietnam.

A May 1975 *New York Times* article found that, in general, workers who were hardest hit by the recession were the ones most vocal in their opposition. In his article "Wide Hostility Found to Vietnamese Influx," reporter Douglas E. Kneeland wrote,

> Those interviewed in hard-pressed Detroit and Los Angeles, for example, tended to be harsh in their resentment of the newcomers. . . . "People are losing their cars, houses, jobs," said a 35-year-old black auto worker in Detroit. . . . "Let them stay there [Vietnam] until we do something for people here." Another worker commented, "This area is overcrowded now. I don't see why we should sacrifice our jobs and bring in more people. We are not obligated to police the whole world."[30]

Some state governments also had reservations. California, for instance, the location of Camp Pendleton, was home to nearly 1 million unemployed workers. Anxious that California citizens not lose jobs to foreign workers, then Governor Edmund Brown demanded that any aid bill passed by Congress stipulate that jobs be provided first for Americans.

A Changing Public Attitude

By no means was the reaction to the Vietnamese completely negative. Many Americans were willing to shoulder the considerable responsibility of sponsoring them. Others felt a moral responsibility because of the damage caused by the war. And still others saw offering asylum and help as part of the American tradition.

In his *New York Times* article, Kneeland also interviewed Robert D. Vilbiss, a salesman who had been out of work for six months. Despite his own shaky economic situation, Vilbiss felt the United States had an obligation to help the Vietnamese. He cited how the United States had assisted both Hungarians and Cubans who sought asylum when their countries were, like Vietnam, taken over by communism. "'We have received refugees from other countries seeking to get out,' he said. 'We . . . can't deny the same to the Vietnamese.'"[31]

As the immigrants became part of American society, even more people began to adopt Vilbiss's view. Julia Vadala Taft, director of the Interagency Task Force, was well aware of the public's initial negative feelings and concern. Soon, though, she says that opinion began to change.

As soon as the media got there [inside the camps] and started interviewing the families . . . the American people could see . . . that these are living human beings who had gone through [great suffering] and were here seeking freedom and respite and a new life. Well, those [media] stories changed public attitudes. . . . By the end of June [1975] public support began to pick up. The vol-ags had their sponsorship campaigns under way and thousands of sponsors were coming forward."[32]

The immigrants themselves contributed to that change in public opinion. In fact, Taft says they played an invaluable role in changing their fate. "I give credit to the refugees. . . . [They] went to communities all over the country. They worked hard. They were dear people. They were appreciative. They sold themselves [made people like them] and they are still selling themselves today."[33]

CHAPTER FOUR

Early Challenges to Adjustment

[While in the camp we were told] that to survive in the United States was not easy; there were other ethnic groups from Asia and Europe who had been in America for decades, there was competition for the job market, and there were prejudices, tension, and discrimination. Most of us believed we would overcome all obstacles to survive.

—A Vietnamese immigrant waiting in a refugee camp. In *The Boat People.*

Upon arriving in the United States, the Vietnamese achieved their most basic goal: safety. After arriving they faced a more subtle, yet in some ways more difficult, challenge. They had to adapt their ancient culture to their new one.

At the core of that ancient culture are respect, harmony, and loyalty. Family, community, hard work, and education are its highest values. Over the years, conflict with the French, as well as the civil war between the North and the South, had threatened the ancient culture's existence. Yet the Vietnamese outlasted all challenges and preserved their way of life.

The United States presented an entirely new set of demands and obstacles. Early difficulties were many, and, in some cases, deeply threatened all that the Vietnamese cherished.

The family is the central feature of Vietnamese life.

Dispersal Policy

Prior to 1975 Vietnamese immigration was extremely limited. In that year, only about fifteen thousand Vietnamese lived in the United States, and most were either exchange students on temporary visas or the wives of American servicemen. As a result, the Vietnamese who came to the United States during the late 1970s had no community waiting to welcome them. Unlike Italians, who might head for a city's "Little Italy," or Chinese, who could find welcome in a city's "Chinatown," the first Vietnamese arrivals had only each other.

The federal government, determined not to saturate any one geographic region of the country with the newcomers, initially dispersed the immigrants across the country. Vietnamese were relocated to all fifty states; eighty-one were even sent to Alaska.

Although this might have been a good policy from the government's perspective, it was devastating for the Vietnamese, for whom community is a cornerstone. The dispersal policy directly challenged the immigrants' traditional way of life. In many instances, they found themselves not only the lone Vietnamese, but also the lone foreigners in their new towns. Vietnamese writer Hien Duc Do describes the hardship this created for the new arrivals:

In essence, the Vietnamese were deprived of the emotional, social, and psychological support generated from the extended family and also the support that was generated from shared culture, language, customs, and experience. They became isolated in their new "homes" and had to rely for support on sponsors who did not speak their language, understand their customs, or celebrate their culture.[34]

Equally as important as community is the importance of family. In fact, family may be the culture's central value. Family stretches back over many generations. Ancestors are honored and revered. Their concept of family extends beyond the American nuclear family, to include grandparents, aunts, uncles, and cousins. Although family loyalty is undeniably a strength, it also caused problems for the new arrivals.

Keeping the Family Together

A surprising number of Vietnamese managed to flee with their large, extended families intact. Breaking up these families into smaller units, as sponsorship often did, was very painful for them. Writer Gail Paradise

Kelly tells the story of one caseworker assigned to Camp Pendleton who tried to photograph a family in order to place them with separate sponsors. The family, who had made their living as fishermen, numbered more than thirty people.

The family at first refused to come out of the barracks to be photographed until the head of the family was promised that only one photograph would be taken of everybody. The family came out of the barracks and huddled together, refusing to budge as the caseworker tried to take pictures of them in groups of threes and fours. The caseworker…was trying to take pictures of households for the purpose of splitting the family up for resettlement.[35]

Housing and employing so many people in one location was difficult, though. Competition for affordable apartments caused friction. In some cities, Vietnamese were housed in low-rent projects designed for other minority groups, including African Americans and Hispanics. Often, this engendered resentment among the Vietnamese's non-Asian neighbors. Even as many Americans welcomed the Vietnamese into their churches and neighborhoods, others viewed the immigrants with suspicion and even animosity. For example, in Oklahoma City, when the first Vietnamese began to move into low-income neighborhoods, friction arose. Interviews with residents revealed fear of both communism and of an alien culture. One local woman said, "I don't like them people being in here. They have some strange beliefs. . . . I don't let my kids play down

Paying Their Dues

Among the many challenges the first arrivals faced was the perception that they received preferential treatment from the government. This perception caused resentment among other groups who were also struggling economically and socially. In The Vietnamese Americans, *Hien Duc Do gives an example of friction that occurred in North Carolina between newly arrived Vietnamese and African Americans who had lived in the region for generations.*

African Americans felt the Vietnamese refugees received preferential treatment in a lower-income housing track called Grier Heights. Vietnamese were seen as allowed to move into the housing project at the expense of . . . African Americans who had been presumably on a waiting list for a long time. African Americans resented the fact that [said one resident] ". . . We had to work hard for what we have. Now you want to give the Vietnamese all the things we have worked for." . . . African Americans were expressing the underlying understanding that a new group has to pay its dues like all the other groups before it can harvest and enjoy the benefits from this country [the United States]. . . . As Americans who have . . . suffered continual discrimination, African Americans begrudged [that] . . . the federal government was willing to provide for Vietnamese who were strangers. . . .

there [where the Vietnamese lived] and I don't even walk down there after dark. Can't we do something about them?"[36]

A Tonal Language

Adding to some Americans' paranoid perception of the Vietnamese was their strikingly different language. Language in fact may have provided the new arrivals' largest challenge. Vietnamese is a tonal language, meaning that the tone in which a word is spoken determines its significance and meaning. The speaker's voice—rising, falling, breathy, creaky—makes the difference between words that are spelled identically. For example, in Vietnamese *ma* may mean ghost, check, but, tomb, horse, or rice plant, depending on the tone in which it is spoken. In English, on the other hand, tones are not part of the language except for emphasis. Moreover, Vietnamese rules of grammar contrast sharply with English.

For these reasons, English, a notoriously complicated language for anyone to learn, was difficult for the Vietnamese. The situation was equally challenging for those who wished to teach and employ them.

Lack of Communication

Well-educated Vietnamese had the least trouble improving on or learning English. And, because language is imperative to success in a host country, their path to employment and independence was the smoothest. Surveys conducted by the U.S. Office of Refugee Resettlement found that the employment rate for Vietnamese immigrants who spoke English with some competency was about 51 percent. For those who spoke no English, the rate was only 6 to 9 percent, depending on where they lived.

In general, the boat people, who had often received little formal education in Viet-nam, belonged to the latter group. For these immigrants, literacy had never before been necessary to earn a living. Learning English ultimately became one of the most difficult aspects of their adjustment to urban American life. One researcher writes, "Those who left Southeast Asia in 1978 or later differ demographically from those who came out at the fall of Saigon in 1975. The more recent refugees arrived with fewer material resources, personal contacts in the United States, education, job skills, English language skills, and westernization experience in general."[37]

The immigrants themselves agree. One of these later arrivals described his challenge

Bilingual community service leaders teach recent arrivals how to use the supermarket where all the signs are in English.

this way: "When I got to America, I did not read my own language [Vietnamese] so good, but I was a farmer. In this place, [America] I have to read [to] eat. That makes it hard for me but it makes me force [myself] to learn."[38]

For the elderly, learning English was especially difficult because language acquisition generally becomes more difficult with age. In the case of older Vietnamese immigrants, there was the added hurdle of resistance to the new culture and homesickness for the old homeland. Their inability to communicate made older immigrants dependent on younger members of the family, which in turn undermined the elders' positions as heads of the household. As a result, many felt isolated and helpless. Ba Thei, an elderly woman who fled rural South Vietnam with her husband and grown children, told an interviewer, "I have lots of barriers. If I have to fill out papers, I cannot. I also am unable to answer the phone. . . . If I'm sick accidentally, I don't know what to do because we are always home by ourselves, my husband and I. . . . I'm kind of sad. . . . If people speak a little, I can understand only a very little, not a lot."[39]

Work Equals Respect

The language barrier also caused problems for immigrants searching for employment. Finding work was of utmost importance to the new arrivals. The combination of hard work, patience, and the drive to succeed even has its own phrase in Vietnamese: *tran can cu*. Traditionally, being able to support a family was the foundation of re-

Terror in the Supermarket

The Asian American Almanac, *edited by Susan Gall and published in 1995, gives this example of some of the confusion new arrivals faced.*

New Vietnamese immigrants have had to adjust to cultural contrasts . . . that could make a harrowing experience out of even a routine trip to the supermarket. In Vietnam, product labels show only pictures of the product or its source, unlike the range of images U.S. citizens have come to expect from creative packaging. A Vietnamese mother visiting a Safeway in Oklahoma was horrified to discover pictures of babies on jars of Gerber's baby food and had to be reassured that U.S. citizens do not practice cannibalism.

spectability. Thus, the new arrivals were eager to find employment not only to support themselves, but also to establish their independence. In addition, many immigrants were eager to raise the funds necessary to bring over the family members they had left behind in Vietnam.

As willing as they were, all newcomers had difficulties at first. Even those with connections and education had to make compromises. Many immigrants who had been professionals in Vietnam found that their credentials were not transferable or accepted in the United States. Doctors, attorneys, and teachers, among others, were asked to undergo retraining, a process that might take years. One immigrant, who had worked as an attorney in Vietnam, describes the difficulty he faced in pursuing his career once he reached the United States:

I liked practicing law in Vietnam. It was a lot different here [the United States]. . . . At first, when I came here, I wanted to continue with my career in law, but my English wasn't good enough. . . . Besides, I couldn't afford to attend a law school; it costs

too much. Anyway . . . I had other things that were more important and which I had to worry about. My wife was still in Vietnam and my energy was spent trying to bring her over here. I needed to work as much as possible to save money to pay for the fees and the paperwork.[40]

Others were steered into jobs totally unrelated to their past careers. Historian Paul James Rutledge described the situation facing another immigrant.

Tho Van Tran was a pilot in the South Vietnamese Air Force. . . . When he first arrived he was given a job in a greenhouse in Little Rock, Arkansas

In Vietnamese culture a woman runs the home. Moving into the American style of women working outside the home proved stressful for many Vietnamese families.

for two dollars an hour, and within a year moved to Oklahoma where he worked as a welder's helper for minimum wage. He labored during the day and worked toward a college degree in the evening.[41]

Saving Face

For Tho Van Tran, as for many upper-class immigrants, the move to the United States initially resulted in downward mobility. Although they willingly accepted jobs below their ability, most suffered a loss of status from white-collar to blue-collar work. For the Vietnamese, who place a high value on respectability, this was a demoralizing experience.

For the boat people, who generally lacked the skills necessary to land high-level jobs, government assistance or low-paying work were the only avenues available. Many members of this group were former farmers, fishermen, or tradespeople. Although these refugees did not suffer a loss of prestige and power, they faced the difficult adjustment from a rural to an urban lifestyle.

Changing Roles

Another shift in employment patterns occurred when Vietnamese women began to take jobs outside the home. This was a major role change, and initially it caused considerable upheaval within families. In Vietnam, the woman ran the home. Although

From Barrister to Busboy

The jobs Vietnamese took when they first arrived in the United States were often a drastic step down in status and pay. Yet the Vietnamese willingness to take whatever employment was available was a major factor in their rapid economic climb. In From Vietnam to America, *Gail Paradise Kelly contrasts some of the jobs the immigrants held in their homeland to the ones they consented to do upon arrival in the United States.*

Job Held in Vietnam	Job Held in U.S., 1976
Air Force Colonel	Newspaper deliveryman
	Night Watchman
Medical Doctor	Limousine Driver
	Dish Washer
Bank Manager	Bank Janitor
Professor of Literature	Furniture Assembler
Three Star General, Army	Maitre d'

many worked side by side with their husbands on farms or in fishing, only the man of the family held outside employment. His role was that of provider, head of the house, and decision maker.

In the United States, these traditional roles quickly changed. Widows, as well as women who had been separated from their husbands during their escape, or whose husbands had been detained by the new Vietnamese government, had little choice but to work. For some intact families, it was often easier for women than men to find employment, especially in the service sectors or in low-paying jobs. For others, women took outside employment while their husbands received training for new jobs, or went to college.

Although this role change was necessary, the clash of old and new lifestyles caused stress in many families. Traditional patterns of authority were upset. Roles that had been unquestioned became unclear. Not being able to provide for their families was demoralizing and depressing for many men. A Vietnamese man in New Orleans, who had six children, commented, "It is hard for me to say that my wife makes more money than I [do]. She would not work if we were in Vietnam, but I have no choice here."[42]

Many Vietnamese teenagers and young adults living at home also began to work. In Vietnam, they would automatically have turned over any money they earned to the family. In the United States, however, where children generally have their own money and spend it as they wish, young immigrants began to assert their independence. They needed their paychecks for clothes, gas, movies. This change in roles caused more friction.

A Different Kind of School

In the Vietnamese hierarchy of values, education closely follows family and community. Few people are more revered than teachers, and few activities are more encouraged than study. *Tran hieu hoc*, or love of learning, is at the heart of the culture.

Vietnamese schools, however, were quite different from the ones in America. In Vietnam, teachers were strict authority figures, and the methods of learning were primarily memorization and repetition. Out of respect, children rarely questioned a teacher. Listening and observing were the behaviors most encouraged. Vietnamese children who suddenly found themselves in noisy, interactive American classrooms were often bewildered.

An eleventh-grade Vietnamese boy in Texas described his confusion this way.

It took me a long time to learn that I am supposed to talk back to [question] my teacher. My father got very angry with me for doing this, but I will not do well in school if I sit passively and do not ask questions. Most of the time, I act like an American at school but don't tell my father. At home, I follow the Vietnamese customs. It makes it hard, but I am doing okay like that.[43]

Most Vietnamese children adapted well to their new schools. However, for children who had received little or no formal education in Vietnam, school remained difficult.

In Vietnamese schools children learned to listen and observe. When they came to America they had to learn the new skills of speaking out and questioning the teacher.

The Emotional Toll of the War

Problems with school and changing family roles challenged all immigrants. The first arrivals carried yet another burden—this one both weighty and invisible. Years of living in a war zone, with day-to-day survival an uncertainty, had left deep emotional scars. Many of these painful experiences were repressed during the months it took to escape and to be resettled, a survival mechanism that enabled the immigrants to deal with the immediate problems of migrating.

Once the immigrants had taken up some semblance of a new life, however, large numbers found themselves rocked by depression. Many of the common factors contributing to this depression included grief, isolation, and economic stress. One of the unique problems faced by the Vietnamese immigrants, however, was survivor guilt. According to Hien Duc Do, this syndrome caused a good deal of mental stress among the earliest arrivals. He describes survivor guilt this way:

> The . . . syndrome occurs when a refugee, especially one who has experienced a tremendous amount of trauma while trying to escape Vietnam and has lost family members . . . asks why he or she has survived and not the other members. This creates a

tremendous amount of psychological pressure for the survivor because he or she feels inadequate and unworthy of living. He or she can imagine hundreds of reasons why other people were more deserving to live and many reasons why he or she should have perished.[44]

Survivor guilt, depression, and acute anxiety were all mental-health issues for the first arrivals. The federal government, however, emphasized meeting the immigrants' physical needs, including being settled and finding work, rather than their psychological needs. Moreover, the Vietnamese were reluctant to use the mental-health services that were available. The health care system in America was difficult to understand and utilize for those who knew little English. Working two or more jobs, as so many did, made medical appointments difficult. Perhaps the biggest deterrent, though, was a cultural issue. Mental-health care was unknown in Vietnam. Admitting the need for help was a stigma. It betrayed traditional Vietnamese values and resulted in disgrace. A Vietnamese woman living in Wichita, Kansas, expressed her feelings this way, "I have bad dreams and I wake up crying but I cannot tell anyone. I feel guilty that I lived when some of my family died, but I just try to be quiet and go on. No one wants to hear me complain. That would not be good."[45]

Expectation Versus Reality

Another traditional value that caused the immigrants problems was their great respect for hierarchy. Vietnamese take care to demonstrate respect to their superiors—the government, teachers, and the heads of households. Complaining out loud is frowned upon in Vietnamese culture, and confronting someone of authority—whether that person be a teacher, a doctor, or a police officer—is rare.

Surprisingly, this desire for agreement and accord caused problems upon arrival in the United States. Some immigrants, for example, agreed to resettlement situations that did not work out. On other occasions,

New Kid on the Block

In his memoir Catfish and Mandala, *Andrew X. Pham tells what it was like being a part of a newly arrived family in Louisiana:*

[S]chool] was dull, particularly because we didn't speak English. . . . I got into scrapes regularly with kids calling me Viet Cong. I fought with every kid who wanted to try Kung Fu. . . . For Dad, life in America wasn't easy. In Vietnam, he was a teacher and an officer with two thousand men under his command. In Shreveport, he was a janitor in an industrial plant. His back was killing him. He'd injured it in the labor camp. And for Mom, America was a lonely, scary place. . . . Mom rarely left the house. She didn't know anyone and she didn't speak a word of English.

Still Remembering

In his book Hearts of Sorrow, *social researcher James A. Freeman included these thoughts from an elderly Vietnamese American man. Highly successful in America, his heart is still in his home country.*

Of course we must love our land, our country where we were born, where we have our own parents, where we have the tombs of our ancestors. The fact that we had to leave our country was something against our will. When we left our country, we turned our heads and cried. And after many years of living in America, we still remember our country. . . . Just because we have a comfortable life in America, we'll not forget our country.

church sponsors thought the immigrants wanted to convert to their religious denomination, only to discover the Vietnamese had no such intentions. And sometimes, the jobs provided were a mismatch. These and other misunderstandings hindered the first immigrants' assimilation efforts.

Historian Darrel Montero argues that unrealistic expectations by both the Vietnamese, sometimes in an effort to please, and by their sponsors were at the root of many misunderstandings. He writes:

The problems faced by the Vietnamese could have been minimized if the refugees had had a more realistic perception of their sponsors and if the sponsors had been given a better idea of the problems involved in the task they assumed. Sponsors often did not understand the refugees' expectations. Questions of employment availability often were pursued only superficially, and language problems were greatly underestimated.[46]

The long list of obstacles the refugees faced made their adjustment difficult. But although they abandoned their native country, the Vietnamese never abandoned their values. Instead, within their homes, they adhered to tradition, passing those values on to their children. At the same time, they publicly adapted, doing whatever they felt necessary to succeed. Including the new, but never excluding the old—that is the Vietnamese way.

CHAPTER FIVE

Making It in America

First and foremost, learn to be virtuous. Then learn to be literate.

—Vietnamese proverb. On the web site www.boatpeople.com.

Family, community, education, and hard work—a formula for success in a new country. In fact, these are the very values Americans themselves have traditionally believed ensure success. Because these values are also cherished by the Vietnamese American community, these immigrants are, despite their many early challenges, succeeding in American society.

A Second Migration: Establishing a New Community

Within six months of the closing of the last transitional camp, the refugees were on the move again. The government's dispersal policy had fragmented kinship systems, the extended family units that were an essential source of comfort and support. As a result, once they oriented to life in their new country, thousands of Vietnamese left their initial placements. This second, internal migration shifted populations from rural towns to urban centers. For example, in New York State, many immigrants moved from upstate communities into New York City. The cities, they felt, offered a wider variety of jobs, better schools, interaction with other Vietnamese, and more extensive social services. Frank Jao, a Vietnamese American developer in California, explains, "The Chinese, the Japanese, the Italians and the Jews grouped together when they came to the U.S. There seemed to be no reason why the Vietnamese wouldn't follow the same tradition."[47]

This relocation gave the Vietnamese a supportive base, both emotionally and economically. It also reunited separated family members. Andrew X. Pham, whose family had been sponsored by a church in Louisiana, said:

> Nine months after we came to America . . . Mom couldn't handle being the only Asian family in town and Dad wanted to be closer to his brothers who had settled in California . . . we loaded a U-Haul. . . . We bolted through Texas, New Mexico, Arizona, and right into sunny California, as close to Vietnam as you can get, my uncle had claimed.[48]

The Pham family was one of many to choose California. Nearly 45 percent of the total Vietnamese American population were drawn to that state's sunshine and mild winters, which reminded them of Vietnam's tropical climate. California also offered ample jobs for unskilled labor, especially in San Francisco's Silicon Valley, an area just south of San Francisco Bay. Additionally, a core settlement of Vietnamese, made up primarily of those who had been in Camp Pendleton, was already located in Orange County near Los Angeles.

This Vietnamese farmer originally settled in Louisiana but later moved to Southern California to reunite with his family and the larger Vietnamese community located there.

Strength of Community

Relocation was actually the first step in the Vietnamese weaning themselves from their sponsors. As the sponsorship program came to an end in the mid 1970s, the immigrants themselves gradually took over the responsibility of helping newcomers. In 1975 they formed the first Mutual Assistance Associations. These private, nonprofit organizations were run by Vietnamese communities and funded by both private and government money.

The Mutual Assistance Associations worked to promote assimilation. Some of the services they supplied, and, in fact, continue to supply, included helping immigrants secure employment, teaching language classes, and providing tutoring for everything from reading a contract, to buying groceries, to driving a car. Because these organizations employed Vietnamese, new arrivals saw them as safe, reliable sources of support. As a result, the Mutual Assistance Associations' efforts were successful.

As the Vietnamese become increasingly secure, the nature of the associations continues to change. For example, many are now associations of professionals (including physicians, technology experts, and scientists) that sponsor conferences for members to network, learn about the latest developments in their fields, and receive updates on the changing laws and requirements of their professions. Many cities with large Vietnamese populations even have their own Vietnamese Chambers of Commerce, comprising business owners and other professionals seeking to promote economic development.

Helping Each Other

The Vietnamese immigrants also help one another on a one-to-one basis. Rather than simply enjoying their own good fortune, they follow their traditional proverb, *An man tra dao*, "If one receives a plum, one must return a peach." In one example in Oklahoma City, a Vietnamese mechanic with relatively good English skills established himself as a valued employee at a car repair shop, then persuaded his supervisor to hire other immigrants who possessed good mechanical skills but spoke little English. The first mechanic then served as an interpreter for the new hires, and worked extra hours without compensation to help them.

Another example of one-on-one community support among the Vietnamese includes the immigrants themselves assuming the role of sponsor for friends and relatives wishing to emigrate from Vietnam. As the numbers of economically successful Vietnamese steadily increase, this sponsorship has become the primary route to America for the continuing influx of immigrants.

Taking on roles that were originally filled by American sponsors and government agencies is clearly an outgrowth of the Vietnamese belief in family and community. Banding together in various communities, the refugees have created a network of small and large associations aimed at meeting the needs of new transplants. These communities are beneficial in two ways. First, they offer emotional support to new arrivals. Second, they provide financial support to immigrants having trouble establishing themselves. In fact, in recent years the communities have become a financial necessity. Federal and state support for refugees began to wane during the late 1970s and has continued to decline. A refugee arriving in 1980 could count on up to three years of government assistance, but by 1982 that time limit had been reduced to eighteen months.

Murals depicting village life in Vietnam can be found throughout "Little Saigon." They help the community preserve traditional values while still participating in the larger American culture.

Economic Progress

This community cooperation and mutual aid have been integral to the economic progress the Vietnamese have made since their first arrival. As author James Freeman notes, "Perhaps never before in history have so many refugees succeeded economically so fast and so well."[49]

Contributing further to that success is the Vietnamese work ethic. Hard work and optimism are important to them, and for the majority of Vietnamese immigrants finding a job that feeds the family is the first goal; finding the right job is second. Agreeing to work night shifts, or to work at employment considered undesirable, as store clerks in crime-troubled neighborhoods, for example, has translated into substantial employment opportunities. In many families, husbands, wives, and older children all work, often more than one job at a time. Andrew X. Pham says of his largely immigrant neighborhood during the late 1980s:

Saving for the American dream was the immigrant's religion. The Lees, two doors down from us, ran a convenience store out of their one-car garage. . . . Mrs. Nguyen next door took in tailoring work at night and ran a day-care center. Old Mrs. Chen, a Chinese-Vietnamese grandmother who lived with her children . . . operated an underground catering business. Every day she cooked dinner for some thirty neighbors who moonlighted at second jobs and didn't have time to cook.

One of our white neighbors, Mr. Slocum, once asked Dad, "Why are you people killing yourselves working around the clock like that?"

Dad replied, "How can you kill yourself when you are already in heaven?"[50]

Pham's parents, too, ascribed to the community's hard-working philosophy. His mother ran a hairdresser business out of their living room. His father studied for hours each day to earn a degree in computer programming, a two-year program he crammed into nine months. During the time Pham's father was unemployed, the family accepted government assistance.

Like the majority of Vietnamese immigrants, however, the Phams' time on welfare was short. By 1980 only five years after the first influx, 72 percent of the Vietnamese community received no monetary assistance from the federal government. By 1990 the median household income of Vietnamese Americans had climbed above the national average. Considering the narrow range of opportunities they had when they first arrived, many experts see that success as remarkable.

This new prosperity, though, was not shared by all. The poverty rate also remains higher than average, and among Asian Americans as a whole the Vietnamese average income is lower than the norm. Those who are the most successful are the early, elite immigrants. For many of the uneducated boat people, life remains an economic struggle.

Yet as a whole, the Vietnamese American population continues to make signifi-

Victoria Nguyen survived a relocation camp, illness, and life in America as a single mom to graduate from college at age 40 with a degree in biology.

An Excused Absence

On January 10, 1986, William J. Bennett, secretary of education, gave a speech to the City Club of Cleveland. He told an anecdote about the emphasis the Vietnamese put on education. In the Vietnamese home, Bennett said, homework is so sacred it comes before meeting a member of the president's cabinet. Quoted in James Paul Rutledge's The Vietnamese Experience in America, *an excerpt from Bennett's speech reads,*

I had the opportunity to go to California to talk to the Vietnamese League of Orange County. The audience I spoke with was made up entirely of Indochinese, new Indochinese American citizens. There were the Boat People, not the first wave but the second wave; these were people who were poor, fishermen and tailors and tanners who left in those boats, crowded in those boats, and came to the United States. They are not native English speakers. . . . When I gave the talk the hostess for the evening apologized to me for some empty chairs. She said, "I'm sorry, Mr. Secretary, but there are some parents who work with their children every night on homework and thus could not come to hear you." I said the secretary of education grants excused absences for those parents, that's okay.

cant progress. The gap between those early, privileged immigrants and the later arrivals has narrowed over the past twenty-five years. As a second generation of immigrants with excellent English skills, fewer cultural barriers, and successful role models enters the workforce, the numbers of middle class continue to grow.

A Drop of Blood

The success of the Vietnamese is a result of not only their work ethic and cohesive communities, but also of the closeness of their families. In Vietnam families often worked together as a unit—whether farming, fishing, or running small businesses. This practice translated well in America, where many Vietnamese have gone into business for themselves. Grocery stores, convenience stores, restaurants, boutiques, beauty shops, and vegetable-supply businesses are some of the more popular establishments. In a culture that believes in the proverb "a drop of blood is better than an ocean of water," running a business with one's extended family has proven a highly successful venture.

One example of a refugee who blended the Vietnamese reliance on family with the American belief in taking advantage of opportunity is Mr. Liem. A former fisherman whose brother sponsored his move in 1978, today, Liem lives on the West Coast. When he and his family first arrived, they began to grow vegetables in the backyard of his family's apartment, which was provided through the Public Housing Authority. At first they sold only to their neighbors, but in time Liem got a permit to sell in a local farmers market. He says,

I brought my vegetables to the market, and . . . after two years of this, we can save some. . . . Then we decided to have a fish truck. I borrowed some [money] from my brother. . . . During my work as a fish merchant, my income was better. . . . Later, if we make a little bit more, we won't receive any help from the Department of Social Services. . . . When my sister came to America, she did as I am doing now. She and her family grew vegetables. Now they have two Vietnamese grocery stores. [51]

Although Liem succeeded more quickly than others, his willingness to work long hours, take initiative, and adapt his skills to new circumstances are all representative of the traits that have made the Vietnamese a growing force in the American economy. Between 1982 and 1987, the U.S. census listed a 414 percent increase in businesses privately owned by Vietnamese Americans. Although these businesses originally catered mostly to Vietnamese customers, during recent years a growing awareness of, and appreciation for, Asian culture has begun bringing in non-Vietnamese clientele as well.

"Little Saigon"

Many of those businesses are located in Orange County, California, an area south of Los Angeles, not far from where Camp Pendleton was located. Between 1980 and 1990 the Vietnamese population in Orange County increased by more than 271 percent, making them the fastest-growing ethnic group in that area. In fact, the last name Nguyen far outnumbers the name Smith in many Orange County phone books. So many Vietnamese Americans live and run businesses in the county that a stretch between the towns of Westminster and Garden Grove has been dubbed "Little Saigon."

When Vietnamese first began settling in Orange County during the late 1970s, the area was a run-down, undesirable sector comprising mainly vacant lots and small stores. In a scenario that has been repeated in inner cities and depressed areas across the country, this soon changed. The Vietnamese took advantage of the low rents to establish a community. With loans from Mutual Assistance Associations or from prosperous relatives, they redeveloped the area. Homes, temples, medical offices, and family-run businesses soon replaced the blighted buildings and trash-strewn lots. Buildings were painted the pinks, blues, and greens of old Saigon. Vietnamese-language newspapers appeared, along with street signs in Vietnamese. As the area began to thrive, more Vietnamese moved in, more entrepreneurs were attracted, and more investors were willing to supply capital. Today, the once all-but-abandoned strip in Orange County is a prosperous community. According to a *Time* magazine article,

Between 20,000 and 50,000 Vietnamese flock each weekend to 800

Vietnamese-Americans have built strong privately-owned businesses in America.

shops and restaurants [in Orange County's Little Saigon], buying herbal medicine and dining out on snail-tomato-rice-noodle soup. In the mornings, people may attend Buddhist ceremonies in makeshift temples; in the evenings they can applaud Elvis Phuong, who, complete with skintight pants and sneer, does [Elvis] Presley Vietnamese-style.[52]

Although the appeal of the district is still primarily to the Vietnamese themselves, this is changing. For example, in 1988 the Westminster Redevelopment Agency acknowledged the area's commercial potential by officially designating it the "Little Saigon Tourist Commercial District." Signs on nearby freeways now direct tourists to the district.

A Growing Political Voice

Despite their success in so many other areas, the Vietnamese have been slow to organize politically. As new arrivals in an initially hostile country, they concentrated on getting an economic footing rather than try to gain political influence. The earliest immigrants, particularly those who had American connections and could speak English, became important voices in their communities. They often acted as translators and facilitators for less educated and less prosperous immigrants. Working along with government and volunteer agencies, they became local leaders, influential in running the Mutual Aid Associations and in securing state and federal funding for their communities' needs.

An example of one such leader can be found in Tony Lam, who fled Vietnam in

1975. A successful businessperson, his accomplishment was noted in the *The Asian American Encyclopedia*:

The 1992 elections were a turning point for Westminster's Vietnamese community. Two Vietnamese American candidates, Tony Lam and Jimmy Tong Nguyen, ran for positions on Westminster's City Council. Lam, a local restaurateur and community activist, won a seat by 132 votes, making him the first Vietnamese American to be elected to political office in the United States.[53]

Today, Asian Americans represent a potentially important and wealthy political voting bloc. Many of the children and grandchildren of those who arrived during the earliest waves of immigration now have enough financial stability and cultural savvy to enter politics. As these new generations come of age, the focus of the Vietnamese community is on leaving the pain and bitterness of the past, and moving toward a prosperous American future. The importance of a political voice is clear because they still face many challenges, including racism, the language barrier, youth criminal activity, and family left behind in Vietnam.

In an effort to deal with those challenges, young Vietnamese have begun to step forward with a political confidence and sense of empowerment the last generation lacked. College campuses, where Vietnamese are significantly represented, are often the setting for this growing awareness. Writer Hien Duc Do describes what has been happening in California over the last decade:

Since the early 1990's, Vietnamese American university and college students have organized annual conferences at the University of California. . . . These conferences focus on issues regarding their ethnic and cultural identity, personal and professional responsibilities, and their roles in American society. These groups are consciously trying to create a forum for members of this generation— those

Education Versus Entertainment

A Vietnamese legend explains the people's ideas about learning versus amusement. In The Vietnamese Experience in America, *author Paul James Rutledge relates the tale:*

The Vietnamese explain their love of learning with a story of unknown origin about a farmer's wife who took a sheet of rice paper away from her grandson after he had written on the paper. She reverently burned the paper and the calligraphic writing on it instead of allowing her grandson to keep the paper and make a kite out of it, feeling that to use the paper in such a frivolous way after it had been the carrier of ideas and thoughts would be to desecrate it.

The Asian Garden Mall is at the heart of the "Little Saigon Tourist Commercial District."

who came here at a very young age, are being educated at America's elite colleges and universities, and are intending to stay in the United States—to articulate their ideas, and to implement their vision of how the Vietnamese American community should develop.[54]

In addition to working together, Vietnamese have begun to politically band with other rapidly growing immigrant groups, including other Asian Americans and Latinos. A growing sense of solidarity with other immigrants and minorities, as well as with other Vietnamese, bodes well for this next generation's political clout.

SEARC

Yet another powerful example of increasing political strength is the Southeast Asia Resource Action Center (SEARAC). Founded in 1979 by a group of Americans concerned over the continuing refugee crisis, SEARAC helped to found and promote the first Vietnamese community self-help organizations—the Mutual Assistance Associations. It has since grown into an advocacy organization with long-term goals. Its mission statement says,

SEARAC's vision is to raise the voice of Southeast Asian Americans, and to thereby increase their participation in the shaping of domestic policy. SEARAC is expanding its advocacy mandate to cover legislation and policies at federal and state levels, such as welfare reform and naturalization, that could have harmful effects on Southeast Asian Americans.[55]

One of SEARAC's key functions is working with community associations and providing them with leadership training and information. SEARAC also works closely with the National Alliance of Vietnamese American Service Agencies. A highly visible and effective organization, SEARAC looks forward to future accomplishments. As one of its former presidents, the refugee Le Xuan Khoa explained, "For many years, we [Southeast Asian immigrants] have been considered a problem. Now we want to be part of the solution."[56]

Education

The growing economic and political presence of Vietnamese Americans cannot be separated from their faith in education.

Here, too, they have faced challenges and setbacks. They have not succeeded to the extent of some other Asian American groups. For example, only about 21 percent of Vietnamese adults hold bachelor's degrees, close to the national average, but far below the 41 percent for Asian groups as a whole. Yet, as is the case with economic and political gains, educational achievement is on the rise.

Success in school is a focus in most Vietnamese American homes, where nightly homework sessions are required and where older siblings assist younger. A recent study done in the San Diego, California, area showed how closely Vietnamese American adolescents and their parents share this belief in education. The study notes that 90 percent of adolescents want to attain at least a bachelor's degree, a response echoed by 87 percent of their parents. In fact, the San Diego study goes on to observe that the children of immigrants have even higher expectations for themselves than their parents do. Sixteen

Many young Asian Americans are well-educated and interested in raising political awareness.

Vietnamese parents encourage and support their children's success in school.

percent of Vietnamese parents interviewed expect their children to earn graduate degrees, but 69 percent of the adolescents intend to earn those degrees.

Like many new Americans before them, the Vietnamese see schooling as their chief hope not only of material success, but also of winning respect. Education brings financial self-reliance. It is also a way of winning prestige. A 1990 study of Vietnamese students on California college campuses showed that the most popular majors were engineering and computer science, fields that generally guarantee good-paying jobs. A Vietnamese immigrant explains, "I . . . tell my kids that people value those with an education, with degrees and certificates. Asian people with black hair, black eyes, and tan skin cannot survive in a strange country if they don't try hard to get a good education. This society still has plenty of discrimination; education is the best way to get respected."[57]

Living in both a family and a neighborhood that hold the same values is a strong factor in influencing behavior. The cohesiveness of the Vietnamese American community, and its emphasis on cooperation, helps motivate students to achieve. As their parents strive to get ahead in the workforce, the children strive to do well in school. A group of high school students interviewed in Oklahoma City commented on how they view education. One boy said, "The only way to get ahead and to get respect is to make good grades. I get all A's, but so do a lot of students. That's why I also try to win with my science project. It helps me to be respected." One of his peers added, "The best way to learn the American culture is to do [well] in school. I want to be an American and this is the way."[58]

Vietnamese American successes—financial and educational—have been hard won. Yet sustained by tradition, community, and family, this immigrant community has endured and prospered. A 1998 article by SEARAC director Ka Ying Yang summarizes the hopeful vision most Vietnamese have for the future: "Let's march into the 21st century joined by the sense of spirit for community empowerment, economic independence, political activism, intergenerational respect and social consciousness."[59]

CHAPTER SIX

Continuing Challenges

Although we have been at times weak, at times strong,

We have at no time lacked heroes.

— Nguyen Trai, Vietnamese poet. In Cam Hang Truong, *Nguyen Trai: His Life and Achievement.*

Vietnamese have been in the United States for more than twenty-five years, yet they continue to struggle with problems related to their immigration. The breakdown of the extended family, disagreement between the generations, racial tension, mental-health difficulties, and friction over ties with communist Vietnam—all of these are issues that challenge the community today.

Differing Cultures

Among Vietnamese Americans, the clash of old and new has been a particularly difficult problem. Because they fled war and communism and did not leave their homeland ongood terms, many first-generation Vietnamese have never fully acclimated themselves to their new country. Even those who eagerly accepted the challenges and possibilities of their new lives found some American customs alien and destructive.

Perhaps the greatest clash has come over the respect due the older generation. In

Vietnam ancestors are revered. A child's most important duty is to show obedience toward his or her elders. A father's authority extended far beyond that of a typical American father, and included the right to physically punish his children, and to choose whom they would marry; daughters were more restricted than sons. Families expected to continue to live in proximity to one another, even after the children had married and moved into their own homes. Grandparents continued to be contributing members of the household until they died. Children learned all these customs at a very early age, and the sign of a good family was harmony among its members.

Upon arrival in the United States, these time-honored values were immediately tested. Children, who generally learned English more quickly than anyone else in the family, served as translators, taking over the authority role of their parents and grandparents. Language, in fact, remains the greatest point of difference between generations. Vietnamese American children are ten times more likely than their parents to speak, understand, read, or write English. Approximately 44 percent of adult Vietnamese in America still speak no English at all.

This loss of control was the first of many. Questioning authority and valuing economic independence, Vietnamese American children and adolescents challenged many of their parents' and grandparents' values. Although proud of their children's success, many older Vietnamese

Vietnamese American teens often question the values and authority of their traditional parents and grandparents.

became anxious about the growing distance between the generations. They also want, more than younger generations, to return to the old world values, beliefs, and behavior. The authors of *The Boat People* note,

> Parents clearly believe that the past is as important as the present, and, as carriers of their heritage, they work hard to bring its lessons into the present to instill continuity and direction to family life. They have faith that the cultural foundation on which their lives rest will support them through the vicissitudes [ups and downs] of resettlement.[60]

Maintaining the traditions, though, can be difficult as American and Vietnamese cultures often clash. What these parents called discipline in Vietnam is sometimes called child abuse in the United States. Dating, unknown in Vietnam, is widely acceptable, as is divorce, also rare in Vietnam. The American emphasis on the individual replaces traditional communal values. Vietnamese must adjust to their children moving far away for school or employment.

These cultural differences have been difficult to adjust to, especially for senior citizens. Accustomed to being respected, contributing members of the family, seniors sometimes find themselves sidelined to the dependent, peripheral role more common in the United States. Members of this group, who generally have very limited English skills can lead isolated lives. Unable to pass the test for a driver's license, or to navigate public transportation, they tend to stay within their own neighborhoods, often with only other Vietnamese for company. Their children work, and their grandchildren speak English, not Vietnamese, as their first language, a fact that makes communication within the home difficult.

The Second Generation

Vietnamese American children have also suffered from the clash of cultures. Their problems come from having to work out the differences between the two cultures. Growing up with the influence of both cultures, they face the choice of conforming to, or rejecting, their parents' strong expectations.

For many of the younger generation, the difficult situation is exacerbated by the fact that even though the Vietnamese have steadily made economic progress, many still work in minimum-wage occupations. As a result, in 1990 more than 20 percent of Southeast Asian families lived below the poverty level. As their children become increasingly Americanized, this low economic status becomes a source of embarrassment and conflict. Vietnamese adolescents, like most adolescents, want to have stylish clothes and the latest CDs; they want to be able to attend movies and concerts with their friends. Yet traditional Vietnamese culture values work, not entertainment or immediate gratification. Author Min Zhou described the problem this way:

> Today's second generation often finds itself straddling different worlds and receiving conflicting signals. At home, they hear that they must work

Forever in Debt

Vietnamese children learn the importance of family at a very young age. This learning begins at home with parents and grandparents, and it is reinforced by the school, the temple, and other social institutions. The contrast to the American notion of independence and individualism is striking. In The Vietnamese Americans, *Hien Duc Do quotes a proverb about the unconditional love a child is expected to bear for his/her parents:*

Cong cha nhu nui Thai Son, nghia Me nhu nuoc trong nguon chay ra. Mot long tho Me kinh Cha, cho tron chu hieu moi la dao con, or, "The debt we owe our father is as great as Mount Thai Son [a mountain in Vietnam]; the debt we owe our mother is as inexhaustible as water flowing from its source. We must repay [this] debt in order to fulfill our obligations as children."

hard and do well in school in order to move up; on the street they learn a different lesson, that of rebellion against authority and rejection of the goals of achievement. Today's popular culture, brought to the immigrants through the television screen, exposes children to the lifestyles and consumption standards of American society, raising their expectations well beyond those entertained by their parents.[61]

Because the Vietnamese emphasis on tradition simultaneously provides identity and engenders conflict, it is both a strength and a weakness. Although the retention of old values has been essential to the success the immigrants have achieved, it has also driven a wedge between the generations. An elderly Vietnamese woman says,

Here we [older people] need them [younger people] more; they don't need us. In Vietnam, if I wanted to go to the market, I just picked up a basket and went. I didn't need anybody to take us. Over here, I have to wait until the [children] take us. If they don't go, we don't go. This makes me sad, yes. . . . In Vietnam, they obeyed us more. Over here, whenever we say something, they like to argue about it. My husband and I dislike this. . . . Things we consider to be right they consider wrong. . . . Our children do not keep the old traditions.[62]

Mental Health Issues

These conflicts between old and new, elderly and young, affect mental health. Especially among the isolated elderly, depression is a serious problem. Survivor guilt, as well as post traumatic stress disorder, are psychological burdens for many who fled during the late 1970s and early 1980s. Marital conflict, caused by the rapid change in roles men and women experienced after immigrating, is another issue. Youth adjustment problems are yet another concern.

Yet the Vietnamese, like Asian Americans as a whole, continue to underutilize mental health services for several reasons. First, they do not distinguish between illness of the body and illness of the mind. Although they do experience grief and anxiety, most Vietnamese are not accustomed to seeking help from someone who treats only the emotions. Second, Buddhism teaches its followers to embrace suffering as a necessary aspect of life. Thus, individuals strive to cope with their pain. Admitting the need for help is a stigma, and results in the loss of dignity.

The scarcity of services geared toward the Vietnamese is also a problem. Because psychiatry is a relatively new medical field in Asia, Vietnamese counselors are rare. Most counselors are white; few are bilingual, and few have a grasp of Vietnamese beliefs and values. Lack of sensitivity to cultural issues, for example the Vietnamese emphasis on the community rather than the individual, can hamper communication and make treatment difficult. In addition, many poorer Vietnamese are reluctant to take time off from work and have difficulty securing transportation to appointments. As Vietnamese become a more vocal and prosperous part of American society, and as more enter the medical profession, some of these obstacles are lessening. At present however, receiving adequate mental health care remains an ongoing problem.

Gangs

Another ongoing challenge is youth gangs. A *Los Angeles Times* survey published in 1994 reported that 41 percent of Vietnamese living in six California counties believed that gangs and crime were the most serious problems their communities faced. Other cities—Denver and Seattle, for example—where there is a large Vietnamese population share this concern.

A 1993 FBI report traced the gangs' origins to illegal activities in Saigon during the late 1960s and early 1970s. Many of the people involved in these activities, the report says, left Vietnam in the second wave of immigration. Upon arriving in the United States, they joined or formed new gangs.

Statistics are difficult to compile. The number of different gangs, and their membership, is constantly shifting. Also difficult to gauge is what prompts youth to join a gang, although experts do cite a number of possible reasons. First, members of Vietnamese gangs are generally from poor families and unsuccessful in school. Vietnamese parents, accustomed to Vietnamese schools where the teachers are responsible for all learning problems, are not always involved in their children's education, and the parents may be unaware of their difficulties. Lack of English skills only makes the problem worse. Young people who have poor English skills tend to spend their time with other Vietnamese, and in some high schools and neighborhoods the growth of Vietnamese groups leads to tensions with other, non-Asians. Vietnamese youth then may band with one another for protection from verbal and physical harassment.

Another possible cause of gang involvement is the disparity between prosperous, early immigrants and later, less successful ones. Tony Vong, a youth counselor who coordinated a gang-prevention program in California, believes this disparity causes envy, anger, and depression, and may contribute to criminal activity. Says one writer who quotes Vong:

When the newcomers see the thousands of successful and highly Americanized Vietnamese whose families fled their homeland years ago, many feel even more depressed. They enroll in class and they don't understand what's going on. They feel that it makes them look stupid. Then they join gangs or buy guns to prove to people that they are something in the community.[63]

Side by side with their inability to assimilate successfully, Vietnamese gang members have usually experienced a breakdown in their traditional family structure. Traditional parents find it increasingly difficult to understand or communicate with their Americanized children. Vietnamese boys and girls who perceive their parents as too rigid may be drawn to gangs as a way of asserting their independence. Furthermore, the long hours parents have to work leaves their children unsupervised. Madison Nguyen, operations director for a San Jose center that runs gang-prevention programs, says, "Truant kids, unable to communicate with their parents who are too busy working, turn to trouble instead. And the parents' [traditional] model of communication—I talk, you listen, because I'm the parent—becomes the source of resentment for the child."[64]

Other experts, though, suggest that tradition, in fact, is an element in encouraging gang violence. Citing a shooting in which two Vietnamese youths killed another in San Jose, California, following an argument over a girl, counselors said that this retaliation was a way of saving face or maintaining honor. In Vietnam, where citizens are generally unarmed, the conflict might have resulted in a fistfight. In the United States, the consequences were more serious.

Addressing the Problem

Dealing with gangs has been difficult for the Vietnamese community. Crime activity, generally confined to Vietnamese neighborhoods, has often gone unreported. Older Vietnamese, who remember the repression of communism, may not trust the police. Some, having worked so hard to achieve respectability, fear the shame crime brings to their communities. And the traditional emphasis on harmony has made many reluctant to face the conflict.

Recently, however, progress has been made in persuading neighborhoods to meet the problem directly rather than regard it as a shameful secret. In Westminster's Little Saigon, for instance, the first Vietnamese American police officers have joined the force and they serve as translators. They also work to assure the community, particularly the elderly, that the police are there to help, not deceive, them. In other areas, Vietnamese community leaders publicly criticize gang activity. A resident of a Vietnamese neighborhood in Dallas, Texas, reflected a growing attitude when he said, "People who steal and kill are not real Vietnamese. They have broken our trust and do not deserve to be protected by us."[65]

Racial Friction

Despite the widespread concern, the percentage of Vietnamese youth involved in gangs is relatively small. Far more are succeeding, which causes its own set of problems. In the past, observers have pointed to this population as a model of adaptation. Some now see an increasing resentment of success.

This mixed reception is nothing new. When the first Vietnamese arrived in 1975, the positive reaction of many communities was offset by hostility in others. Some of the most violent anti-Vietnamese reactions occurred along the coast of the Gulf of Mexico. Many immigrants who had made their living as fishermen in Vietnam flocked to the Gulf Coast to work on the shrimp boats. The increased competition they provided angered many American fishermen. Making matters worse, the Vietnamese, unaware of local customs and laws, caught fish in the territory claimed by Americans. In 1980 Texas shrimpers burned Vietnamese boats. In 1981 the Ku Klux Klan threatened Vietnamese families by burning crosses in their yards. Dressed in hoods and armed with rifles, the Ku

Trust and cooperation between the Vietnamese community and law enforcement has been greatly enhanced by the hiring of Vietnamese Americans as police officers.

Klux Klan patrolled the Gulf of Mexico as vigilantes. Furthermore, in Mississippi, bumper stickers reading SAVE YOUR SHRIMP INDUSTRY: GET RID OF VIETNAMESE were distributed by American shrimpers.

Education on both sides has eased much of the tension in the South and throughout the nation. Mutual respect has developed over time. Yet racial misunderstanding has not completely disappeared. In 1985 and 1986, for instance, violence against Asian Americans, including Vietnamese, jumped by 50 percent in Los Angeles County. In 1996 Ly Minh Thien, who had just received a master's degree, was found murdered in Tustin, California. The two men who confessed to the crime subsequently wrote the *Los Angeles Times* a letter of racial epithets against Asian Americans.

A *Time* magazine article reporting on the problems of prejudice still faced by Asian Americans, including the Vietnamese, stated,

Whatever the cause, racism in one form or another, subtle or blatantly obvious, plagues many Asian Americans. Sometimes strong biases brought over by the immigrants themselves—including racial prejudice, clannishness, and a reluctance to make problems public—hamper their assimilation into the majority. More often, however, Asians are the victims of discrimination. The very visible success of some Asian immigrants and the power of Asian finance have triggered a backlash.[66]

This very visible success has spurred resentment of high-achieving Vietnamese students. Although this achievement is a result of hard work, as well as strong family and community support, some students have become the object of harassment and even racist remarks. A Vietnamese high school girl reports, "I was called 'fish breath' and it makes me angry. I am not a 'chink' or a 'slant eye.' I do not like being called names. . . ."[67]

One reason for those hostile attitudes, say some observers, is jealousy. Asian Americans, including the Vietnamese, are often considered a model for other Americans (both white and minorities) because those immigrant groups have been very successful in the United States. Holding Asian immigrants up as a model, though, can seem like a criticism of other struggling minorities, which sometimes cause resentment. Hien Duc Do explains,

The model minority myth implicitly and explicitly criticizes other racial and ethnic groups for their own cultural shortcomings by sending the message that in order to succeed, they need to possess similar cultural traits and social values. In other words, if Vietnamese . . . can succeed, then why are other racial and ethnic groups unable to succeed?[68]

Clashes Within the Community

The conflicts the Vietnamese face are not confined to outsiders. Within their own community, the issue of future relations with the Socialist Republic of Vietnam is powerful enough to divide Vietnamese Americans into two camps. Reflecting on the impact of this issue,

Paul James Rutledge wrote, "The one destabilizing influence that remains is politics: politics relating primarily to Vietnam and to the process of establishing relations with the Socialist Republic of Vietnam."[69]

The issue in a contentious one in the Vietnamese community with people solidly favoring one of the two standpoints. In 1999 a video-shop owner in Westminster, California's Little Saigon, hung a picture of Ho Chi Minh and a North Vietnamese flag in his store. For seven weeks, angry anticommunist protesters, both American and Vietnamese American, crowded the sidewalk outside the shop. Tony Lam, the first Vietnamese American to be elected to political office in the United States, did not support the protest, and the restaurant he owned was also picketed. An article in *U.S. News & World Report* related Lam's distress. The authors write, "Lam says he spent $143,000 in legal fees, his business dropped 40%, and he eventually was forced to move to another site. 'I lost my country, and I left behind the bones of my ancestors,' he says, weeping. 'Yet they subjected me to this.'"[70]

Many Vietnamese Americans share Lam's sorrow and confusion. For the younger generation, who have few if any memories of their homeland, the

Some older Vietnamese want nothing to do with the communist government in Vietnam and its treatment of people and will protest against establishing any economic ties with Vietnam.

Agree to Disagree

The generation gap continues to cause conflict in families and in the community as a whole. Young Vietnamese American journalist Thu'y Linh wrote an essay that was published in the San Jose Mercury News *on April 30, 2000, the twenty-fifth anniversary of the fall of Saigon. In it, she addressed her elders about the painful division between young and old. Speaking for her own generation, she wrote,*

Yes, we are young, sheltered from the bloodshed and misery you endured. Yet we understand and respect your hardships. And more importantly, we know that we now reap the benefits of your sacrifices. . . . You are afraid we will forget your struggles, forget how much you have lost and given up through generations of war, poverty and displacement, all in the name of freedom. But no matter how much we disagree, we will never forget. . . .

No community is homogeneous; we Vietnamese are not unique in our divides between the young and old, nationalists and communists, eastern- and western-educated. There are many problems . . . juvenile crime, family disintegration due to generational and language barriers, and domestic violence.

There is much to be done.

Let's not fight among ourselves but direct our energy toward tangible social change. Let's disagree but still share a bowl of pho [noodles] together. . . .

communist-led, economically struggling Vietnam of today is the only Vietnam they know. Understanding their parents' lingering bitterness and grief is difficult. Vu Nguyen, a California college student and journalist, was two months old when his family fled. He recently visited Vietnam for the first time since. "It was a horrible experience," he remembers. "They've got dirt roads, people were burning trash on the sides of the road—I can't believe I came from there."[71] Nguyen sides with those who believe that increasing trade and investment with Vietnam makes sense. These immigrants hope that American involvement will help the cause of political freedom in Vietnam, and maybe even boost the country's chances of democracy.

Many elder members of the Vietnamese American community, though, still primarily identify with the past. To them, the United States has never completely become home. Although they have gone from refugee to immigrant to citizen, some continue to regard themselves as exiles. In fact, some older Vietnamese still cling to the possibility of returning one day. An elderly woman's quote in author Freeman's *Hearts of Sorrow* explains how many of her generation feel. "Our life is a lonely one in America. That's why lots of old people want to return to Vietnam. They dream of fighting the communists, throwing them out, and returning to live out their days peacefully in their homeland. But this is only a dream."[72]

Some immigrants and take a middle-view. A former colonel in the South Vietnamese Army now living in California, immigrant Joe Tran hopes that the next generation will work out a compromise. The father of two highly successful children, he believes that his children will play a crucial role in resurrecting Vietnam. He says, "Someday, I expect my kids and [the communists'] kids to rebuild the country [Vietnam]."[73]

A State of Flux

Conflicts such as these are not new to the Vietnamese. Still relatively new arrivals to this country, the Vietnamese accept that their communities are in a state of dynamic flux. In fact, they welcome the chance for growth and change. In a paper titled "Current Research on Asian-Americans on the Gulf Coast," Dr. Jesse Nash of the University of Michigan notes, "The community . . . because of its strong bonding in communal structures, is not torn apart by these conflicts. The conflicts actually provide a forum whereby the community can make decisions as to its future."[74]

Thus, even as they differ, the Vietnamese seek harmony. Consensus and agreement may be hard won, but they are always the goal. Entering the twenty-first century, the Vietnamese community continues to grow in numbers, visibility, and strength.

CHAPTER SEVEN

The Future

When eating a fruit, think of the person who planted the tree.

—Vietnamese proverb. On the website, www.boatpeople.com.

The Vietnamese have become a vital, increasingly visible part of American society, and their future is promising. Their economic, educational, and political gains continue. Their traditions, sustained through so much adversity, have found a new home in the United States.

More than twenty-five years after the end of the Vietnam War, the relationship between the United States and Vietnam has opened up, making a variety of eco-nomic and cultural exchanges possible. As the bitterness of the past eases and appre-ciation for the Vietnamese heritage grows, the immigrants and their descendants will continue to make valuable contributions to American society.

United States–Vietnam Relations

During the early 1990s President Bill Clinton cleared the way for Vietnam to receive its first international financial aid, ending eighteen years of isolation from the democratic world. In 1994 he announced the lifting of the trade em-bargo and the United States established

In 2000 Bill Clinton traveled to Hanoi, the first U. S. president to visit Vietnam in over 30 years.

diplomatic relationships with Hanoi, opening an embassy there. Then, in 2000 the American government pledged $1.7 million to help Vietnam detect and destroy unexploded land mines left over from the war.

The more friendly relationship between the United States and Vietnam is significant for Vietnamese Americans. Many, especially those of the younger generation, hope that the new diplomacy will lessen misunderstandings between the countries and will help Vietnam develop economically and politically. Further, they see the new relationship as a step toward making their future lives in America more complete. The sense of being exiled from their homeland is ending as they are able to return and communicate with family and friends left behind.

These Vietnamese Americans agree with Clinton, who, in November 2000, visited Hanoi. Speaking at Vietnam National University, he expressed his belief that the lifting of barriers will benefit both countries.

We [the U.S. government] are, in short, eager to build our partnership with Vietnam. We believe it's good for both our nations. We believe the Vietnamese people have the talent to succeed in this new global age as they have in the past.

We know it because we've seen the progress you have made in this last decade. We have seen the talent and ingenuity of the Vietnamese who have come to settle in America. Vietnamese-

Americans have become elected officials, judges, leaders in science and in our high-tech industry. Last year, a Vietnamese-American achieved a mathematical breakthrough that will make it easier to conduct high-quality video-conferencing. And all America took notice when Hoang Nhu Tran graduated No. 1 in his class at the United States Air Force Academy.

Vietnamese-Americans have flourished not just because of their unique abilities and their good values, but also because they have had the opportunity to make the most of their abilities and their values. As your opportunities grow to live, to learn, to express your creativity, there will be no stopping the people of Vietnam. And you will find, I am certain, that the American people will be by your side. For in this interdependent world, we truly do have a stake in your success.[75]

Positive Effects

This improving of United States–Vietnam relations has had several positive effects on the lives of Vietnamese Americans. No longer barred from their homeland up to ten thousand Vietnamese a month have gone back since 1994. Many are second generation or left when they were still children. They return to visit relatives, to teach their own children about their heritage, or to discover their roots. Although it is more than a quarter of a century since the first Vietnamese fled, the older immigrants have never forgotten the pain of leaving against their will. Despite their children's many successes, that pain remains part of their legacy. The chance to freely reconnect with their first country is deeply comforting.

In addition, Vietnamese are taking advantage of new economic opportunities. Many travel there as representatives of their American employers; the United States is now the eighth-largest foreign investor in Vietnam. Others take the responsibility of travel and expenses on themselves. The Viet Kieu, for instance, is a growing group of successful young professionals who return to Vietnam as entrepreneurs and temporary residents. The benefits to both the Viet Kieu and the family they left behind are obvious. Says a writer for *The Asian American Almanac*, "They [Viet Kieu] can often benefit professionally from family connections, and, with the reciprocity characteristic of the Vietnamese family, some bring along money to help their families establish small businesses of their own."[76]

Thus, the establishing of Vietnamese American relations has benefited the immigrants both emotionally and economically. Although many of the older generation continue to hope for the overthrow of communism, younger Vietnamese look forward to a future of increasing closeness between the two countries.

Veterans Making Peace with the Past

Among Americans, too, old animosity is fading. Today, hundreds of U.S. veterans of the Vietnam War, assisted by funds from both the private and public sectors, are working to rebuild Vietnam. Working as individuals, or as representatives of organizations like the Vietnam Veterans of America, they are helping to recover the remains of the tens of thousands of missing Vietnamese soldiers. The veterans are building orphanages and medical clinics (and ensuring that these organizations continue to be funded), equipping schools with books and supplies, and working on numerous other projects.

These efforts benefit not only the Vietnamese, but also the American servicemen and servicewomen who fought in the war. A former Marine explained how the experience helped him to heal. "Since my trip to Vietnam, the old images of the war are still with me, but have somewhat faded and are in the past. Now when I think of Vietnam I have new images: smiling children . . . a beautiful country, the people at peace. It makes my heart feel good."[77]

For the majority of Vietnam War veterans, the memory of the war remained a nightmare even years after it was over. Returning to the scene of the war, and working to repair its destruction, helps these veterans make peace with their experiences. In turn, these humanitarian efforts foster a compassion for what many Vietnamese immigrants endured and overcame. Such efforts help increase understanding, mend old hostility, and build a feeling of partnership on both sides.

Celebrating Their Culture

Until recently, the issues of assimilation took priority over participating in cultural traditions. The Vietnamese have worked hard to fit in but now younger Vietnamese—second generations and those who immigrated as children—feel secure enough both to fully participate in the larger American society and to begin sharing their heritage with that society. As a result, Vietnamese American communities increasingly serve as places where Vietnamese and non-Vietnamese alike can enjoy Vietnamese culture. The popularity of Vietnamese cuisine, for instance, is evidenced by the rapid growth of Vietnamese restaurants. And specialty food stores in Vietnamese neighborhoods are patronized by many non-Vietnamese who have discovered the pleasures of spring rolls, chicken with lemongrass, and soup pho (a flavorful broth with noodles).

Another example of the celebration of Vietnamese culture is the increasing popularity of the festival of Tet, the Vietnamese New Year and most important holiday. Beginning on the first day of the first month of the lunar calendar, Tet generally falls between January 19 and February 20. In Vietnam, families gather for several days of feasting and ancestor worship. As the start of a new year, and a celebration of the return of spring, Tet symbolizes new beginnings and the rebirth of the culture.

In the United States, Tet is a time of remembering the past while celebrating the new and looking toward the future. According to author Paul James Rutledge, in large Vietnamese American communities in California and Texas, the festivals serve as "the focal points for Vietnamese identity enhancement . . . community cooperation, community leadership building, and cultural preservation."[78] Community organizations, for example Mutual Assistance Associations, use these gatherings to dis-

At a Seattle high school Vietnamese students perform the lion dance as part of the celebration of Tet, the Vietnamese New Year.

tribute information and to make contact with newly arrived immigrants.

Tet celebrations are no longer attended only by Vietnamese. Government officials recognize their significance and make a point of appearing. Businesses and corporations hoping to attract Vietnamese clientele provide sponsorship. As the festivals grow in size, they become a way to showcase Vietnamese culture to the larger society. Participants dress in traditional clothes, and traditional arts, including silk painting, pottery, and flower arranging, are on display. A space is always dedicated to honoring ancestors, where the Vietnamese pray and make offerings.

In recent years these celebrations have developed a distinctly American flavor. A recent Tet celebration in San Jose, Cali-

fornia, drew more than forty thousand people. According to one writer, its attractions sound like a Vietnamese version of a county fair: "food bazaars, games, outdoor concerts, Karaoke contests, ballroom dances, a Miss Vietnam pageant, martial arts competitions, table-tennis championships, Vietnamese fashion shows, lion dances, and Asian chess matches."[79]

For older Vietnamese, the celebration of Tet is a reenactment of all they left behind and still miss. Younger Vietnamese view the holiday more as a symbol. Even as they live Americanized lives, these younger immigrants draw security from their culture's deep roots. Tran Vo, a teenager living in the Midwest, says, "I like the Tet celebration. It is a time when we can party and have a good time together. . . . I know it is important to my parents. I don't understand what it all means, but Tet is a way of just being Vietnamese. For my folks it is a way of remembering. For me it is a way of saying that that's part of me."[80]

The Arts

Enhancing this growing appreciation for Vietnamese culture is its contribution to the arts. Films, music, and literature are all receiving new attention and respect from the American public.

Admiration for Asian American filmmaking in general is especially high. Janice Sakamoto, director of the Media Fund for the National Asian American Telecommunications Association, comments,

> Previous generations of filmmakers were looking outward with stories of the larger community, primarily using a documentary approach. A new generation of filmmakers is looking inward, to stories that are more personal. But the themes are the same— cultural identity, the generation gap, wanting to be American. . . . Films like *Three Seasons* by Tony Bui, a 1999 Sundance Film Festival winner, involve going back to countries like Vietnam or Cambodia. . . . This new generation of young Asian Americans is coming forward, in numbers never seen before, with big, artistic visions.[81]

A 2001 entry in the Sundance Film Festival, the movie *The Green Dragon* was directed by Tony Bui's Vietnamese American brother Timothy Linh Bui. Filmed in both Vietnamese and English, and featuring more than twenty-five Vietnamese American actors, it is the story of a family's arrival at Camp Pendleton in 1975. The film makes the story of that immigration available to a wide-screen audience for the first time, another step toward understanding and respect for the Vietnamese experience.

Likewise, Vietnamese music, both traditional and modern, is also making its mark. Recordings of classical Vietnamese music are now available everywhere. Contemporary Vietnamese singers, such as the popular Khanh Ha, perform in both the United States and Canada. And the musical *Miss Saigon*, which tells the story of the last days of American involvement in Vietnam, enjoyed a long run on Broadway and is now performed in cities across the country.

Vietnamese literature is also being enjoyed by a larger audience. Vietnamese poetry is being translated and published, allowing Americans to appreciate yet another facet of Vietnamese culture. An increasing body of work by boat people has made their harrowing experience available to the American public. And more Vietnamese folktales are making their way into bookstores and libraries. Stories about Vietnamese dragons, fairies, mythical tigers, and Vietnamese legends—including *The Golden Slipper*, a Vietnamese Cinderella tale, *Why the Rooster Crows at Sunrise*, and *In the Land of the Small Dragon*—now delight American as well as Vietnamese children. In turn, American picture books are being translated into

Tony Bui (second from the right) attends a press conference with the actors in his film, "Three Seasons."

Vietnamese. This crosscultural exchange exposes children to the pleasures of each culture's literature, another step toward to future understanding and respect.

Stereotype?

Some critics argue that the current interest in Vietnamese culture is superficial, however, and does not reflect real understanding of this group's many, widely varied traditions. A recent article in *Asian Week* reported that many Vietnamese living in southern California's Little Saigon feel the news media focuses too much on their food, festivals, and crime. Leaders complained that the news perpetuated stereotypes, that of the hard-working, "nerdy" student, for example. In the case of gangs, the leaders feel the media sensationalized the problem and provided erroneous information. As a result, they asked newspapers to feature more in-depth articles that would foster a true understanding of their culture, rather than easy, and sometimes harmful, stereotypes.

Some people, though, claim the stereotypes are not overly damaging. Although there is no doubt that most Americans have a good deal to learn about the Vietnamese, many leaders are elated by growing trends. They see the gradual weaving of Asian culture into the everyday fabric of American life as positive. Assimilation is a long process, they argue, and Bill Wong, publisher of an Asian American news website, comments, "I'd rather be on the radar screen than ignored."[82] Wong, along with many experts on assimilation, believes that a growing understanding of a culture almost inevitably increases its acceptance. They hope that in the future, this understanding will translate into even less prejudice against the Vietnamese.

Continuing Cooperation

The Vietnamese continue to make their economic mark on American society. Here, too, their traditional ideals translate well. From the beginning, the Vietnamese have collectively pooled whatever resources they had to rent housing, to begin a business, or to help one another's children through school. No matter how long the Vietnamese have lived in the United States, they continue to support one another.

One example can be found in the success the Vietnamese have found as fishermen in southern California. Setting up in the fishing business requires assets few individual Vietnamese have. Yet through cooperation, the Vietnamese have all but taken over the industry in that area. In his study of this group, Craig Thoburn of UCLA explains how the Vietnamese adapted old values to new circumstances:

> Significant cultural traits that allowed Vietnamese to raise enough money to buy boats include "other-orientedness," industriousness, and thrift. Extended families pooled resources and lived together in cramped houses and apartments to raise enough money to purchase a boat. . . . In short, they help one another. A Vietnamese skipper who runs across a school of fish or shrimp will radio his compatriots to come join him. This distinctly un-Darwinian [the theory of survival of the fittest] behavior is an anomaly [exception] in this country's [America's] highly competitive commercial fishing industry.[83]

Working as a group, Vietnamese fishermen are willing to take lower wages than many Americans, and to assist one another when catches are poor, thus sustaining business for all.

Another example of the Vietnamese willingness to cooperate can be found in the many associations and alliances they continue to form. The first neighborhood-based Mutual Assistance Associations still help new immigrants. Yet the concept has expanded in proportion to Vietnamese success. Organizations like the Vietnamese Professional Alliance pool their substantial resources to fund scholarships and provide assistance to needy families. The Vietnamese American Science and Professional Engineering Society, a national organization, not only offers professional support to its members, but also sponsors conferences where such topics as political issues, community action, and the quest for a dual, Vietnamese and American identity, are explored.

One organization, the Vietnamese American Science and Technology Society (VAST), created in 1990, is a professional organization with a mission statement that typifies the kind of concern the Vietnamese show one another. The members of VAST are Vietnamese American as well as Vietnamese residing overseas, and one of the society's objectives is to modernize and rebuild Vietnam. Other objectives include the following:

• Develop mutual technical support, assistance and understanding among Vietnamese science-technology professionals, particularly in Vietnam-related issues

• Provide educational and training assistance to the Vietnamese and other Indochinese…

• Outreach to students and youngsters of Indochinese origin in vocational training, career guidance, employment and family counseling

• Strengthen the interaction and communication with other professional organizations to work on issues and problems of common interest

"A Vital, Vibrant Part of the System"

In 1997 Thang Nguyen Barrett, who was born in Saigon and arrived in the United States as a teenager, became the first Vietnamese American judge. While noting how humble this distinction made him feel, Barrett went on to say his appointment is proof to all Vietnamese Americans "that this is their system, that this is their state and that this is their nation; that they can be a vital, vibrant part of the system and their opportunities and goals can be achieved."[84]

Certainly, problems remain. The average Vietnamese American household income still hovers below the American average. The Vietnamese divide into every economic class. Upward mobility continues to be difficult, especially for those with poor English skills. Conversely, successful Vietnamese have to

Traders, Not Invaders

Lan Nguyen, who was born in Hanoi in 1974, grew up listening to her parents' stories about the terrible war years. Lan, however, associates the United States with books rather than bombs. Interviewed by Carol Clark in the CNN.com article, "Wartime Ghosts Haunt Vietnamese-U.S. Relations," a piece on Vietnamese-American relations twenty-five years after the war, Lan talked about her commitment to bridging the gap between the two countries.

Today Lan [Nguyen], 26 . . . is studying for a master's degree in finance at the Fisher Graduate School of International Business in Monterey, California, and her goal is to return to Hanoi and work for a U.S. company. "Most Vietnamese companies are state-run and they don't work very well," Lan said. "I'm more comfortable with American corporate culture. You can talk to the boss about what you think. You can give suggestions rather than just follow what they tell you."

Lan is one of the movers and shakers in the dynamic post-war generation of Vietnam—where more than half of the population was born after 1975. . . . For these young Vietnamese, war is only stories and photos. They have inherited the tenacity and drive that helped Vietnam defeat bigger and more powerful enemies. But they view non-Vietnamese as traders, not invaders. They want to take their place in the global economy, and they see the U.S. as key.

deal with resentment for their achievements, both from the white majority and from other struggling minorities.

Yet in innumerable ways, Vietnamese immigrants and their descendants have shown that they can adapt and can make their own way in a new country. The initial resentment that the first arrivals faced has been eased by their example of hard work and discipline. The Vietnamese desire for

Outcasts No Longer

The Amerasian Homecoming Act, signed in 1987, is an agreement between the American and Vietnamese governments. For the first time, both governments allocated money to help people of mixed heritage (Asian and American) emigrate. Under the act, Amerasians do not have to pay for the lengthy paperwork necessary to leave, and they receive counseling and support for the many complications that can arise, including child custody and the eligibility of accompanying family members. The experience was difficult but, as usual, most Vietnamese met the challenge with determination. In the internet article, "Nho's Proposal to Improve Conditions in the ODP (Orderly Departure Program) Camp," Nho Thi Nguyen, an Amerasian now living in the United States, described her journey here.

When the U.S. soldiers withdrew from Vietnam, they left thousands of their Amerasian children behind. For several years the mothers of these children had lived in Vietnam taking care of the children by themselves. . . . The U.S. government wanted to give these Amerasian children a chance to live in the land where their fathers were born. . . . Many Vietnamese Amerasian families decided to move . . . when the U.S. government offered the deal. . . .

Before my family left for America, our relatives and friends had told us that America is a land of prosperity, freedom, and plenty of food. . . . Our relatives had cautioned us regarding how big America is and the challenge of living in a society with such high technology so different from what we were used to in Vietnam. . . . The cities were so big that we could easily become lost. . . . This would be a major problem for my family, because we couldn't speak English. . . .

The trip to America was the most challenging my family had ever made. . . . We'd never before been in an airplane because the expense for the eight of us was about $6,400. This amount would take my mother years of hard work to earn. However, our flight . . . was paid for by the Orderly Departure Program (ODP) [the federal program overseeing immigration during the 1980s]. After we had lived in America for a year or so and had jobs, we repaid ODP for our flight expenses.

A Vietnamese girl proudly displays her trophy for academic excellence and her certificate written in both English and Vietnamese.

self-sufficiency has silenced fears that their population would put a strain on public assistance funds. In every community where they have established themselves, the Vietnamese have proven their desire to be contributing, independent citizens.

In addition, the early arrivals have worked out some of the cultural obstacles to assimilation. A woman's role as wage earner is now generally accepted. Girls, in fact, are as highly encouraged as boys to do well in school and to continue on to college and a career. The rigid, traditional roles of father, mother, and child have loosened. Although most Vietnamese continue to live together in urban neighborhoods, those who can afford it have begun to move into suburbs. Vietnamese Americans have become leaders in business and have established a political voice. They have made valuable contributions in the fields of science and technology. The numbers of Vietnamese holding public office are growing. This increasing political voice helps raise public concern about issues the Vietnamese face, including immigration law, small-business legislation, and the fight against prejudice. In all these areas, the early arrivals have acted as role models. They have set the standard for future generations to follow and to exceed.

The terrible circumstances that first brought the Vietnamese to the United States have turned out to be their new home's good fortune. In the relatively brief time they have been here, the Vietnamese have made their mark. Sharing their culture's enduring strengths, they have broadened America's appreciation of diversity. As they continue to transform themselves, they are transforming America.

NOTES

Introduction

1. Quoted in Darrel Montero, *Vietnamese Americans: Patterns of Resettlement and Socioeconomic Adaptation in the United States*. Boulder, CO: Westview Press, 1979, p. xv.

Chapter One: Why They Left the Home They Loved So Much

2. Quoted in David Chanoff and Doan Van Toai, *Portrait of the Enemy: Vietnam, a Portrait of Its People at War*. New York: I. B. Tauris, 1996, p. 43.
3. Quoted in Mary Beth Norton, David M. Katzman et al., *A People and a Nation: A History of the United States, Fourth Edition*. Princeton, NJ: Houghton Mifflin, 1986, p. 969.
4. Duong Van Mai Elliott, *The Sacred Willow: Four Generations in the Life of a Vietnamese Family*. New York: Oxford University Press, 1999, pp. 314–15.
5. Quoted in Norton et al., p. 969.
6. Fox Butterfield, "How South Vietnam Died," *New York Times Sunday Magazine*, May 25, 1975, p. 40.
7. Quoted in *Reporting Vietnam, Part 2*. New York: Literary Classics of the United States, 1998, p. 489.
8. Quoted in James A. Freeman, *Hearts of Sorrow: Vietnamese American Lives*. Stanford, CA: Stanford University Press, 1989, p.15–16.
9. Elliott, *The Sacred Willow*, p. 390.

Chapter Two: In Search of Safety

10. Andrew X. Pham, *Catfish and Mandala*. New York: Farrar, Straus and Giroux, 1999, pp. 69–70.
11. Quoted in Paul James Rutledge, *The Vietnamese Experience in America*. Indianapolis: Indiana University Press, 1992, p. 21.
12. "Journey to Freedom Land," *Time*, May 19, 1975, p. 10.
13. Quoted in Rutledge, *The Vietnamese Experience in America*, p. 16.
14. Elliott, *The Sacred Willow*, p. 428.
15. Quoted in Scott C. S. Stone and John E. McGowan, *Wrapped in the Wind's Shawl: Refugees of Southeast Asia and the Western World*. San Rafael, CA: Presidio Press, 1980, pp. 70–71.
16. Quoted in Freeman, *Hearts of Sorrow*, p. 274.
17. Quoted in *Freeman, Hearts of Sorrow*, p. 281.
18. Elliott, *The Sacred Willow*, p. 457
19. Quoted in Rutledge, *The Vietnamese Experience in America*, p. 24.
20. Hien Duc Do, *The Vietnamese Americans*. Westport, CT: Greenwood Press, 1999, pp. 30–31.

Chapter Three: Welcome to Freedom Land

21. Quoted in Rutledge, *The Vietnamese Experience in America*, p. 16.
22. Quoted in Freeman, *Hearts of Sorrow*, p. 424.

23. "Journey to Freedom Land," *Time*, p. 10.
24. Quoted in Larry Engelman, "Light at the End of the Tunnel: How 130,000 Refugees Found New Homes in America Before Christmas in 1975." *Vietnam Magazine*, December 1996, www.shwvhome.html.
25. "Journey to Freedom Land," p. 13.
26. Pham, *Catfish and Mandala*, pp. 165–66.
27. Quoted in Freeman, *Hearts of Sorrow*, p. 370.
28. Quoted in Engelman, "Light at the End of the Tunnel."
29. Quoted in Nathan Caplan, John K. Whitmore, and Marcella H. Choy, *The Boat People and Achievement in America: A Study of Family Life, Hard Work, and Cultural Values*. Ann Arbor: University of Michigan Press, 1992, pp. 14–15.
30. Douglas E. Kneeland, "Wide Hostility Found to Vietnamese Influx," *New York Times*, May 2, 1975, p. 18.
31. Kneeland, "Wide Hostility Found," p. 18.
32. Quoted in Engelman, "Light at the End of the Tunnel."
33. Quoted in Engelman, "Light at the End of the Tunnel."

Chapter Four: Early Challenges to Adjustment

34. Do, *The Vietnamese Americans*, p. 41.
35. Gail Paradise Kelly, *From Vietnam to America: A Chronicle of the Vietnamese Immigration to the United States*. Boulder, CO: Westview Press, 1977, p. 92.
36. Quoted in Rutledge, *The Vietnamese Experience in America*, p. 107.
37. Caplan et al., *The Boat People*, p. 24.
38. Quoted in Rutledge, *The Vietnamese Experience in America*, p. 116.
39. Quoted in Freeman, *Hearts of Sorrow*, p. 372.
40. Quoted in Do, *The Vietnamese Americans*, p. 83.
41. Rutledge, *The Vietnamese Experience in America*, p. 80.
42. Quoted in Rutledge, *The Vietnamese Experience in America*, p. 84.
43. Quoted in Rutledge, *The Vietnamese Experience in America*, p. 92.
44. Do, *The Vietnamese Americans*, p. 72.
45. Quoted in Rutledge, *The Vietnamese Experience in America*, p.106.
46. Montero, *Vietnamese Americans*, p. 31.

Chapter Five: Making It in America

47. Quoted in Howard G. Chua-Eng, "Strangers in Paradise," *Time*, April 9, 1990, p. 33.
48. Pham, *Catfish and Mandala*, p. 189.
49. Pham, *Catfish and Mandala*, p. 191.
50. Freeman, *Hearts of Sorrow*, pp. 384–86.
51. Quoted in Chua Eng, "Strangers in Paradise," p. 33.
52. Franklin Ng ed., *The Asian American Encyclopedia*. New York: Marshall Cavendish, 1995, p. 1,631.
53. Do, *The Vietnamese Americans*, p. 115.
54. Southeast Asia Resource Action Center, "From IRAC to SEARAC— The Story of an Evolving Organization," www.searac.org.
55. Southeast Asia Resource Action Center, "From IRAC to SEARAC."
56. Quoted in Caplan et al., *The Boat People*, p. 121.

57. Quoted in Rutledge, *The Vietnamese Experience in America*, p. 93.

58. Southeast Asia Resource Action Center, "From IRAC to SEARAC."

59. Caplan et al., *The Boat People*, p. 122

Chapter Six: Continuing Challenges

60. Min Zhou, "Straddling Different Worlds: The Acculteration of Vietnamese Refugee Children," http://migration.ucdavis.edu, p. 14.

61. Quoted in Freeman, *Hearts of Sorrow*, pp. 372–75.

62. Quoted in Ken McLaughlin, "Vietnamese Gangs Now Profit from Gun Sales, California Police Say," Knight Ridder Tribune News Service, October 7, 1993, p. 2.

63. Quoted in Jessie Mangaliman and Nam Nguyen, "Gangs Atop Bay Area Vietnamese List of Worries," *Mercury News*, October 8, 2000.

64. Quoted in Rutledge, *The Vietnamese Experience in America*, p. 112.

65. "Strangers in Paradise," p. 33.

66. Quoted in Rutledge, *The Vietnamese Experience in America*, p. 95.

67. Do, *The Vietnamese Americans*, p. 119.

68. Rutledge, *The Vietnamese Experience in America*, p. 142.

69. Mike Tharp, "Divided by Generations," *U.S. News & World Report*, July 17, 2000, p. 2.

70. Quoted in Tharp, "Divided by Generations," p. 1.

71. Quoted in Freeman, *Hearts of Sorrow*, p. 379.

72. Quoted in Tharp, "Divided by Generations," p. 3.

73. Quoted in Rutledge, *The Vietnamese Experience in America*, p. 150.

Chapter Seven: The Future

74. Quoted in "Text of Clinton's Speech in Vietnam," *USA Today*, November 17, 2000, www.vinsight.org/2000news.

75. Susan Gall, ed., *The Asian American Almanac: A Reference Work on Asian Americans in the United States*. Detroit, MI: Gale Research, 1995, p. 174.

76. Quoted online at www.topvietnamveterans.org.

77. Ng, *The Asian American Encyclopedia*, p. 1,635.

78. "Tet for Tat in San Jose," *AsianWeek*, February 2001, www.asianweek.com/2001.

79. Rutledge, *The Vietnamese Experience in America*, pp. 137–38.

80. Helen Zia, *Asian American Dreams: The Emergence of an American People*. New York: Farrar, Straus and Giroux, 2000, p. 276.

81. Olivia Barker, "The Asianization of America," *USA Today*, March 22, 2001, p. 2.

82. Craig Thoburn, "Southern California's Boat People," ISOP—The Newsletter of UCLA International Studies and Overseas Programs, May 1998, p. 4. www.isop.ucla.edu/intercom.

83. Quoted online at www.vastvn.org.

84. Quoted in Rodney Foo, "Barrett Becomes First Vietnamese-American Judge in California," Knight Ridder/Tribune News Service, February 26, 1997, p. 1.

FOR FURTHER READING

Olivia Skelton, *Vietnam: Still Struggling, Still Spirited.* New York: Benchmark Books, Michael Cavendish, 1998. Well-written, highly informative account of Vietnam from past to present.

M.Stanek, *We Came from Vietnam.* Niles, IL: Albert Whitman, 1985. The true story of the Nguyen family, who were among the boat people and now live in Chicago.

Gloria Whelan, *Goodbye Vietnam.* New York: Knopf, 1992. A novel about thirteen-year-old Mai and her family, who fled Vietnam on a dangerous sea voyage.

The CNN site "Vietnam at 25" is a fount of information, maps, interviews, photos, video clips, and documents. www.asia. cnn.com/SPECIALS/2000.

WORKS CONSULTED

Books

Nathan Caplan, John K. Whitmore, and Marcella H. Choy, *The Boat People and Achievement in America: A Study of Family Life, Hard Work, and Cultural Values.* Ann Arbor: University of Michigan Press, 1992. A comprehensive, readable study based on five years of research on Southeast Asian refugees.

David Chanoff and Doan Van Toai, *Portrait of the Enemy: Vietnam, a Portrait of its People at War.* New York: I. B. Tauris, 1996. An account of the Vietnamese conflict from the viewpoints of both North and South Vietnam.

Hein Duc Do, *The Vietnamese Americans.* Westport, CT: Greenwood Press, 1999. A short, readable history of the Vietnamese Americans, with emphasis on the problems facing them today.

Duong Van Mai Elliott, *The Sacred Willow: Four Generations in the Life of a Vietnamese Family.* New York: Oxford University Press, 1999. A successful Vietnamese American author traces her family's roots in this poignant, highly informative account.

E. B. Fincher, *The Vietnam War.* New York: Franklin Watts, 1980. A brief, informative account of the history leading up to the war, as well as its long-reaching consequences.

James A. Freeman, *Hearts of Sorrow: Vietnamese American Lives.* Stanford, CA: Stanford University Press, 1989. Moving firsthand accounts, spanning experiences from rural Vietnam in the early 1900s through late twentieth century in urban America.

Susan Gall, ed., *The Asian American Almanac: A Reference Work on Asians in the United States.* Detroit, MI: Gale Research, 1995. Succinct account of Vietnamese culture, along with contemporary challenges and successes. Excellent photos.

Susan and Timothy Gall, eds., *Junior Worldmark Encyclopedia of the Nations.* 2nd ed. Vol. 9. Detroit, Michigan: Gale Group, 1999. Excellent guide to the countries of the world; all the important facts are in an easy-to-use format.

Gail Paradise Kelly, *From Vietnam to America: A Chronicle of the Vietnamese Immigration to the United States.* Boulder, CO: Westview Press, 1977. A thorough exploration of the first wave of refugees and their experiences in the four U.S. transitional camps.

Darrel Montero, *Vietnamese Americans: Patterns of Resettlement and Socioeconomic Adaptation in the United States.* Boulder, CO: Westview Press, 1979. A study of the early years of resettlement, and the unique, emerging pattern of Vietnamese American adaptation.

Franklin Ng, ed., *The Asian American Encyclopedia.* New York: Marshall Cavendish, 1995. An excellent reference, with comprehensive coverage of the Vietnamese American community.

Nguyen Ngoc Ngan, *The Will of Heaven: A Story of One Vietnamese and the End of His World*. New York: E. P. Dutton, 1982. Memoir by a South Vietnamese who was imprisoned in a reeducation camp and later escaped to the United States.

Mary Beth Norton, David M. Katzman et al., *A People and a Nation: A History of the United States, Fourth Edition*. Princeton, NJ: Houghton Mifflin, 1986. A comprehensive textbook with excellent coverage of the war and its effect on the United States.

Andrew X. Pham, *Catfish and Mandala*. New York: Farrar, Straus and Giroux, 1999. An account of a bicycle trip through contemporary Vietnam by a young man who left when he was a child. Highly descriptive.

Reporting Vietnam, Part 2. New York: Literary Classics of the United States, 1998. A harrowing collection of news stories filed during the Vietnam War.

Paul James Rutledge, *The Vietnamese Experience in America*. Indianapolis: Indiana University Press, 1992. An extremely useful overview of both the refugee experience and Vietnamese culture.

Scott C. S. Stone and John E. McGowan, *Wrapped in the Wind's Shawl: Refugees of Southeast Asia and the Western World*. San Rafael, CA: Presidio Press, 1980. A collection of primary accounts by refugees—why they left, how they survived, and their hopes for their children and themselves.

Nancy Viviani, *The Long Journey: Vietnamese Migration and Settlement in Australia*. Melbourne, Australia: Melbourne University Press, 1984. Primarily about the Vietnamese experience in Australia, yet provides added insight into why and how the refugees left Vietnam.

Helen Zia, *Asian American Dreams: The Emergence of an American People*. New York: Farrar, Straus and Giroux, 2000. The daughter of Chinese immigrants gives personal witness to dramatic political and personal changes she has seen. Excellent for exploring issues facing Asian immigrants and refugees at the dawn of the twenty-first century.

Periodicals

Olivia Barker, "The Asianization of America," *USA Today*, March 22, 2001.

Fox Butterfield, "How South Vietnam Died," *New York Times Sunday Magazine*, May 25, 1975.

Howard G. Chua-Eng, "Strangers in Paradise," *Time*, April 19, 1990.

George Esper, "Evacuation from Saigon Tumultuous at the End," *New York Times*, April 30, 1975.

Rodney Foo, "Barrett Becomes First Vietnamese-American Judge in California," Knight Ridder/Tribune News Service, February 26, 1997.

Douglas E. Kneeland, "Wide Hostility Found to Vietnamese Influx," *New York Times*, May 2, 1975.

Jessie Mangaliman and Nam Nguyen, "Gangs Atop Bay Area Vietnamese List of Worries," *Mercury News*, October 8, 2000.

Bill Nichols and Jack Kelley, "The Asian-ization of America," *USA Today*, March 22, 2001.

Mike Tharp, "Divided by Generations," *U.S. News & World Report*, July 17, 2000.

Time, "Journey to Freedom Land," May 19, 1975.

Time, "The Agony of Arrival," May 12, 1975.

Internet Sources

Dan Biers and Murray Hiebert, "Finding Their Voice," Far Eastern Economic Review, December 7, 2000, www.feer.com.

Carol Clark, "Wartime Ghosts Haunt Vietnamese-U.S. Relations," http://asia.cnn.com/SPECIALS/2000/vietnam.

Scott McKenzie, "Vietnam's Boat People: 25 Years of Fears, Hopes, and Dreams," http://asia.cnn.com/SPECIALS/2000/vietnam.

Ken McLaughlin, "Vietnamese Gangs Now Profit from Gun Sales, California Police Say," Knight Ridder/Tribune News Service, October 7, 1993. www.galegroup.com.

Jason Ma, "Poll Gauges Vietnamese Americans' View of Media," *AsianWeek*, Thursday, April 27, 2000, www.asianweek.com.

Timothy J. Min II, "Legal History of Asian-American Discrimination & the Illegal Campaign Funds Inquiry," *American Jurist*, www.wcl.american.edu.

Nho Thi Nguyen, "Nho's Proposal to Improve Conditions in the ODP Camp," www.louisville.edu.

Southeast Asia Resource Action Center, "From IRAC to SEARAC—The Story of an Evolving Organization," www.searac.org.

"Tet for Tat in San Jose," *Asian Week*, February 2001, www.asianweek.com/2001.

"Text of Clinton's Speech in Vietnam," *USA Today*, November 17, 2000, www.vinsight.org.

Craig Thoburn, "Southern California's Boat People," *ISOP*—The Newsletter of UCLA International Studies and Overseas Programs, May 1998, www.isop.ucla.edu/intercom.

Min Zhou, "Straddling Different Worlds: The Acculteration of Vietnamese Refugee Children," 1999, www.ucdavis.edu.

Websites

Veterans Working in Vietnam (www.topvietnamveterans.org). A website dedicated to helping Vietnam veterans recover from the trauma of the Vietnam War.

Vietnamese American Science and Technology Society (www.vastvn.org). Provides support, assistance, and understanding for Vietnamese professionals working in science and technology.

INDEX

agriculture
  Agent Orange and, 17
  during French rule, 13
Amerasian Homecoming Act, 98
American Red Cross, 36
Anderson Air Force Base (Guam), 43
Asian American Almanac, The, 73
  on Vietnamese immigrants' cultural adjustment, 58
Asian Americans, 10, 74

Bank of America, 46
Barrett, Thang Nguyen, 97
Ba Thei, 58
Bennett, William J., 70
"boat people," 8
  asylum and, 30, 34–39
  conditions of, 34
  economic struggles of, 69
Boat People, The (Caplan et al.)
  on arrival in America, 40
  on core values, 50
  on generation gap, 80
  on relocation camps, 53
Brown, Edmund, 51
Buddhism
  American concerns over, 51
  communists and, 31–32
  orphanages of, 31
  suffering and, 82, 63
Bui, Timothy Linh, 94
Bui, Tony, 94

California, 66
  concerns of, 51
  settlements in, 10
Cambodia, 50
  China and, 33

communists in, 28
refugees and, 36
war with Vietnam, 32–33
Cam Hang Truong, 78
Camp Pendleton (California)
  fictional story on, 94
  settlements in California from, 51, 66, 71
  as transition camp, 43—48
Caplan, Nathan, 40, 50
Carter, Jimmy, 59
Catfish and Mandala (Pham), 63
Catholicism, 13–14
Chan Vu Ri (Thailand), 49
China
  communism and, 13
  invasion by, 33
Choy, Marcella H., 40, 50
Church World Service, 47
Clark, Carol, 97
Clinton, Bill, 89–90
CNN.com, 30, 97
communism, 12–13
  Cambodia and, 28
  cold war and, 12
  life under, 29–32
  ruthlessness of, 15
Comprehensive Plan of Action, 30
culture
  arts, 94–95
  celebration of, 92–94
  clashes of, 78–81
  community and, 10
  core values of, 50, 53
  old, 11
  respect of elders and, 78–79
  strength of community and, 66–74
  sustaining power of, 89
  Tet festival and, 92–93

work ethic and, 50
"Current Research on Asian–Americans on the Gulf Coast" (Nash), 88

Da Nang (city), 19
domino theory, 13

Eglin Air Force Base (Florida), 43
elderly, 80
  feelings for homeland and, 87–88
  isolation of, 58
Elliott, Duong Van Mai
  on corruption during Vietnam War, 18
  on economy after Vietnam War, 31
  on plight of boat people, 34–35
Esper, George, 21
ethnic Chinese, 33–34

family
  breakdown of, 78
  dispersion policy and, 54–56
  divorce and, 80
  generation gap and, 80–81, 87
  importance of, 10, 50, 70–71
  marriage and, 79, 81
  roles in, 60, 99
  teenagers, 61
Fincher, E. B., 35
  on communist Vietnam, 35
Ford, Gerald
  and fall of Saigon, 23
  on Vietnamese Americans, 8
Fort Chafee (Arkansas), 43
Freeman, James A., 26
  on elderly and homeland, 87–88

on heart of the exile, 64
on leaving Vietnam, 12
on work ethic, 68
French-Indochina War, 13–14
division and, 9
Ho Chi Minh and, 13
Saigon and, 18
From Vietnam to America (Kelly), 24

Garden Grove (California), 71
Geneva Accord, 15
Golden Slipper, The (legend), 94
Green Dragon, The (film), 94
Grier Heights, 56
Guam, 43
Gulf of Thailand, 34

Hanoi, 97
bombing of, 17
U.S. diplomatic relations with, 90
Hearts of Sorrow: Vietnamese American Lives (Freeman), 12
Hien Duc Do
on immigrants, 55
on politics, 73
on preferential treatment, 56
on racism, 85
on Southeast Asian refugee camps, 37–38
on survivor guilt, 62
Hoang Nhu Tran, 91
Ho Chi Minh, 14–16, 86
social justice and, 15
Hong Kong, 26, 35, 36
House Judiciary Committee, 41
Hue (city), 18

Immigration and Naturalization Service, 44
In the Land of the Small Dragon (children's tale), 94

Indiantown Gap (Pennsylvania), 43
Indonesia, 48
Interagency Task Force on Indochina Refugees
acculturation of immigrants and, 52
transitional camps and, 43, 47
International Refugee Services, 43

Jao, Frank, 66
Japan, 14, 36
Johnson, Lyndon B., 16

Ka Ying Yang, 77
Kelly, Gail Paradise
on fear of communism, 24
on immigrant job status, 60
on sponsorships, 45, 47
on Vietnamese family, 55
Kennedy, John F., 16
Khanh Ha (performer), 94
Khao I Dang (refugee camp), 49
Khmer Rouge, 32
Kneeland, Douglas E., 51, 52
Ku Klux Klan, 84–85

Lam, Tony, 72–73, 86
Lan Nguyen, 97
Laos, 50
"Little Saigon," 71–72, 86
"Little Saigon Tourist Commercial District," 72
Lutheran Immigration Service, 43
Ly Minh Thien, 85
Ly Thi Tinh, 20

Malaysia, 35, 48
McGowan, John E.
on dissent after war, 31
McKenzie, Scott, 30
Media Fund for the National Asian American Telecommunications Association, 94

mental health, 78
cultural issues and, 63
depression and survivor guilt and, 81–83
post-traumatic stress disorder, 81
services and, 82
Min Zhou
on children and rebellion, 80–81
Mississippi, 85
Miss Saigon (musical), 94
Montero, Daniel, 64
Mutual Aid Associations, 72
Mutual Assistance Associations, 96
culture and, 92–93
formation of, 66–67
loans from, 71
SEARAC and, 74

Nash, Jesse
on flux in community, 88
National Alliance of Vietnamese American Service Agencies, 75
National Liberation Force, 15
New Economic Zones, 29
New York City, 65–66
settlements in, 10
New York Times (newspaper), 46
on American hostility toward immigrants, 51
on Vietnamese immigrants, 52
Ngo Dinh Diem, 15
Nguyen, Jimmy Tong, 73
Nguyen, Madison, 83
Nguyen Tan Thanh, 15
Nguyen Trai, 78
Nguyen Trai: His Life and Achievement (Cam), 78
Nha Trang (city), 18
Nho Thi Nguyen, 98
Nixon, Richard, 20
North Vietnam
capital city of, 17
communism and, 12

Soviet support of, 16
U.S. trade embargo against,
    30–31

Office of Refugee Resettlement, 50
Oklahoma City (Oklahoma), 55–56
"Operation New Arrival," 45
Orderly Departure Program, 50, 98

Pan Am (airline), 46
Pham, Andrew X.
  on American Dream, 68–69
  on communist takeover of
      Saigon, 25
  on prejudice, 63
  on relocation to California, 66
  on sponsorship, 46
Philippines, 35, 48
  U.S. processing camp in, 43

racism, 63
  clannishness and, 85
  economic concerns and, 84
  other minorities and, 55
Red Cross, 43
Refugee Act, 59
refugee camps
  camps of first asylum, 36
  discontent in, 45
  security screening and, 43–44
  U.S. overseas processing centers,
      42–43
religion, 11, 31–32
Republic of Indonesia, 35
Rodino, Peter, 41
Rutledge, Paul James, 59
  on education, 70
  on employment of immigrants,
      59
  on love of learning, 73
  on Tet celebrations, 92

Sacred Willow, The (Elliott), 18–19

Saigon, 17, 57
  American Embassy in, 8, 19
  European influence on, 18
  fall to communists of, 21–23
  population explosion in, 17–18
Sakamoto, Janice, 94
San Jose Center, 83
San Jose Mercury News
    (newspaper), 98
Seattle (Washington), 10
Silicon Valley, 66
Singapore, 36, 48
Skelton, Olivia
  on a land divided, 14
Socialist Republic of Vietnam, 35,
    85–86
  see also North Vietnam
South China Sea, 21, 25, 34, 50
Southeast Asia, 13
Southeast Asia Resource Action
    Center (SEARAC), 74
South Vietnam
  capital city of, 17
  capitalism and, 13
  United States and
      supported government of, 12,
        15
  troops, 16
  withdrawal from, 20
Soviet Union, 12–13
  cold war and, 12
  North Vietnam and, 16
Stone, Scott C. S.
  on dissent in Vietnam, 31
Sundance Film Festivals, 94

Tan Son Nhut Air Base, 21
Taft, Julia Vadala, 43, 47, 52
Tet Offensive, 19
Texas, 10
Thailand, 35–36, 58
  Cambodia and, 36
  refugee camps of, 49

Thoburn, Craig
  on cultural adaptivity, 96
Three Seasons (film), 94
Thu'y Linh, 87

United Hebrew Immigration
    Assistance Service, 53
United Nations
  definition of refugee, 26
  foreign relocation camps and, 48
  High Commissioner for
      Refugees, 30, 36, 50
United States
  Air Force Academy, 81
  Amerasian children and, 98
  bombing and, 17
  cold war and, 12
  Department of Defense, 16
  dispersal policy of, 54–56
  economic climate, 51
  French and, 14
  Immigration Service, 50
  immigration to, 24–29, 49–50
  moral responsibility of, 41
  protests in, 19–20
  public assistance programs and,
      51
  reactions to immigrants in, 9
  relations with Vietnam, 12, 87
  State Department, 26
  troops of, 16, 20
  U.S. Catholic Conference, 43
  U.S. News & World Report
      (magazine), 86
  U.S. Office on Refugee
      Resettlement, 57

Vgo Van Ha, 30
Vibiss, Robert D., 52
Vietcong, 15, 19
Viet Kieu, 91
Viet Minh, 14
  after fall of Saigon, 22

Vietnam
civil war and, 12, 17
communism and, 12, 29–30
corruption and, 15, 18, 28, 29
division of, 15
economy of, 17–18, 97
French rule and, 13–14
Geneva Accord and, 15
geography, 14
infrastructure of, 17, 29
invasion by
China, 33
Japan, 14
land mines and, 28, 17, 90
United States and
bombing of, 17
relations with, 87–88, 89
troops and, 18
withdrawal from, 20
war with Cambodia, 32–33
Vietnam (magazine), 47
Vietnamese Americans
children, 80, 96
clashes within community of,
85–88
economics and, 95–97
gangs 82–84
generation gap within, 79–80
politics and, 99
racism and, 85
reuniting family by, 65–66
stereotype of, 95
U.S.-Vietnamese relations effect
on, 91
Vietnamese Americans, The (Hein),
56
Vietnamese Americans: Patterns of

Resettlement and Socioeconomic
Adaptation in the United States
(Ford), 8
Vietnamese American Science and
Professional Engineering Society
(VAST), 96
Vietnamese Chamber of
Commerce, 67
Vietnamese Experience in America,
The (Rutledge), 70, 73
Vietnamese immigrants
challenges of adjustment, by
53–64, 78–88
communists and, 20–23, 32
economic progress of, 68–70
education and, 50, 61, 75–77
employment and, 50, 57
families, reuniting of, 65–66
first wave, 24, 27
language and, 11, 56–58
other minorities and, 55–56
politics and, 72–75
ports of first asylum and, 30
racism and, 51, 55–56
as refugees, 26
after resettlement camps closed,
48–50
second wave, 24–25
settlements of, 10, 66
sponsorship, 40, 45–47
study of, 50
survivor guilt and, 62–63
women, 60–61, 99
work ethic and, 58–60
Vietnamese-language newspapers,
71
Vietnamese Professional Alliance, 96

Vietnam National University, 90
"Vietnam's Boat People: 25 Years
of Fears, Hopes and
Dreams" (McKenzie) 30
on refugees, 30
Vietnam: Still Struggling, Still
Spirited (Skelton), 14
Vietnam War, 9
atrocities during, 18–19
emotional toll on Vietnamese
people, 62
protests and, 19–20
U.S. soldiers and, 9
U.S. veterans and, 91–92
Vietnam War, The (Fincher), 35
volunteer agencies (Volags), 43
Vong, Tony, 83

"Wartime Ghosts Haunt
Vietnamese-U.S. Relations"
(interview), 97
Washington, D.C., 19
Westminster (California), 71
Vietnamese American police in,
83
Westminster Redevelopment
Agency, 72
Whitmore, John K., 40, 50
Why the Rooster Crows at Sunrise
(children's tale), 94
Wong, Bill, 95
World War II, 13
Wrapped in the Wind's Shawl
(Stone and McGowan), 31

YMCA (Young Men's Christian
Association), 43

PICTURE CREDITS

Cover photo: CORBIS

AP Wide World Photos , 19, 20, 22, 25, 37, 41, 69, 72, 75, 90, 95

CORBIS, 9, 16, 27, 28, 32, 38, 42, 44, 49, 54, 57, 62, 66, 68, 74, 79, 86, 93

PhotoEdit, 10, 59, 76, 84, 99

UPI, 15, 23

ABOUT THE AUTHOR

Tricia Springstubb holds a degree from the State University of New York at Albany. She is the author of numerous works of fiction and nonfiction for young people. Ms. Springstubb works as a writer-in-residence and as a part-time children's librarian. She currently lives in Cleveland Heights, Ohio, with her family.